MICHAEL WINNER'S HYMIE JOKE BOOK

Michael Winner's HYMIE Joke Book

The Robson Press

First published in Great Britain in 2012 by
The Robson Press (an imprint of Biteback Publishing Ltd)
Westminster Tower
3 Albert Embankment
London SE1 7SP

ISBN 978-1-84954-391-0

10 9 8 7 6 5 4 3 2

A CIP catalogue record for this book is available from the British Library.

Set in Sabon
Printed and bound in Great Britain by
CPI Group (UK) Ltd, Croydon CR0 4YY

CONTENTS

FOREWORD BY MICHAEL WINNER

Humour changes over the years. What used to be considered humorous before political correctness enveloped us would not be considered humorous today because it would be deemed 'insulting'. In this respect, the Hymie jokes which appear in this book are humorous for most of us but considered in dubious taste and not funny at all by some Jewish people who wrote to complain. They are luckily very much in the minority – and in fact most of the jokes were sent to me by Jews. The complainers seem to have the belief that Hymie is a stereotypical Jew that no longer exists and he should not be brought before the world, even in joke form.

The archetypal butt of jokes, if you're American, was the Poles and in England it's largely the Irish. The jokes were perfectly funny but they became unacceptable as time wore on. The fact is that those who suffer persecution or deprivation in their lives make jokes of their situation.

The funniest evening I ever spent was in Northern Ireland at the time of the Troubles. Indeed at a time when their troubles were at their most severe with prisoners defecating in their cells and slaughter going on everywhere. I was there to do an *Any Questions* radio programme. After the programme the BBC executives involved and the panel of *Any Questions* sat on little gold chairs in a hotel room in Belfast. The BBC executives, who were all from Northern Ireland, told a series of jokes that lasted the entire evening. They were some of the funniest stories I have ever heard but could be described as being in appalling taste or having a lack of taste. They drew on the situation in Northern Ireland as it was, including people having their legs shot off, defecating all over their cells, knee-capping each other. Not normally great material for jokes, but told by these Northern Irish people who were living under this great stress it was a relief for them to be able to tell jokes like that, and unbelievably funny. I have never spent an evening hearing funnier stories than on that occasion. But then the Irish have a great sense of humour.

On one occasion I was giving a lecture in Northern Ireland. A lady picked me up at the airport and she said, "My husband wanted to come and greet you but he's marching in an anti-English march." As we went down a certain street she pointed out, "That's the British Embassy. We burnt it down yesterday." On the same visit I was asked to attend a theatre where I was doing my one-man show precisely at 7pm. An interviewer would greet me and familiarise himself with my work, and the show would start half an hour later at 7.30pm. At 7pm I turned up at this theatre, which was totally deserted, it was like a bad day in Hiroshima. Nobody was there or anywhere round the place. Eventually we found an old porter and he let us in the back and showed us to a musty dressing room where we waited. And waited. And waited. There was no sign of anybody in the building. There was no sign that there was going to be an event or that any audience would turn up at all. From time to time my publicity man would look through the curtains at an empty theatre and say, "There's still no sign of anybody coming." This went on until 7.30pm when the interviewer eventually turned up to meet me. I said, "It's 7.30pm and you were insistent I should be here on the dot of seven yet you were not here." "Ah yes," said the interviewer, "we never turn up on time in Ireland, the other person might not be ready." That was a disarming remark if ever I heard one. The show was scheduled to start at 7.30pm. At approximately 7.35pm, my publicist looked through the curtains and said, "Six people have just entered the hall." Thus they trickled in and at 8.15pm, forty-five minutes after the announced commencement of proceedings, the room was absolutely packed and I went on stage before a very appreciative and entertaining audience.

One of the great moments of Jewish humour gone wrong, or actually right, was when the Jewish comedian Jackie Mason performed for Thames Television, *An Evening with Jackie Mason*. Now, if you look at Jackie's jokes carefully they could be considered anti-Semitic. Being a Jew he can get away with it. (He does refer to President Obama as a schwarzer in one of the funniest routines I've ever heard about an American President. The gist of it being if you have to have a schwarzer who's President at least get someone who's black and not someone whose antecedents are largely white.) Anyway on this particular occasion, after it finished, Pamela Stephenson came over to me and said, "No wonder the Jews hate Jackie Mason. He's so anti-Semitic." I said, "Pamela, darling, they don't hate Jackie Mason, the Jews adore Jackie Mason. They pack his theatre shows. He's an absolute hero among the Jewish people." The next day the *Telegraph* said in its review that Jackie Mason told the sort of jokes that they were brought up to believe were extremely bad taste and anti-Semitic, which may or may not be true but they are bloody funny – and most Jews have a sense of humour.

During this particular evening the celebrities in the audience were given questions to ask and that's it. It's not really open to the public. It so happened that in the audience I noticed a man called Josef Buchenwald Behrmann. Josef Buchenwald Behrmann was an actor who very much played on the fact that he had been an inmate of Buchenwald concentration camp – to such an extent that he incorporated the word 'Buchenwald' into his name. So everybody employed him. He was actually a bloody nuisance. I remember Michael Caine saying that on *The Ipcress File* Behrmann insisted on having the same size chair as him. That evening, Josef Buchenwald Behrmann was sitting in the audience wearing a pink tallit (prayer shawl), a pink skullcap and dressed like an old-fashioned Rabbi, except in pink. As Jackie Mason was answering the questions and expecting the set people to come forward with a question, I saw Behrmann put his hand up. Obviously the producers had no idea who he was and thought, "Here's a Jew dressed like a Rabbi, let's give him a question." I could see all the microphones swinging over to Behrmann and the cameras that were not facing the stage turning to him as well. I thought to myself, "I am the only person here who knows what's going to happen now. Let them carry on in their ignorance." So, having called for the question, Josef Buchenwald Behrmann said in his very thick Jewish accent, "Mr Mason, if you were standing in line for the gas chamber in Buchenwald and you were naked and awaiting going to your death, what joke would you tell?" I tell you that brought the audience to its heels. There was a stunned silence. The whole room went into complete shock. Jackie Mason made the mistake of answering. He said, "Really you know this is not that sort of a show. This is an entertainment show. This is not the sort of thing we can discuss in a show like this." And then Jackie Mason made a fatal error. He said, "Who in Buchenwald standing naked in line for the gas chamber would make a joke?" To which Josef Buchenwald Behrmann replied, "I was there, Mr Mason, we did tell jokes. I was there." This left everyone totally stupefied. Jackie really fell to pieces for the next twenty minutes. Both the audience and Jackie had to regroup mentally. Well, the show continued and when it finished I climbed the steps of the auditorium, passing Josef Buchenwald Behrmann. He said, "Tell me, Michael, when you go home, are you driving anywhere near Baker Street?" I said, "No, Josef, I'm not. No." I consider that one of the most memorable evenings in my life and it demonstrated comedy or the lack of comedy very well.

Of course the Jews always have a wonderful world-weary way of using put-downs. My father had a friend called Mr Kay who lived on the sixth floor of a block of flats and Mr Kay said to my father, "You know, my son is always threatening suicide. He's threatening to throw himself out of the window." To which my father replied, "My advice is move to the ground floor."

One of the funniest things that ever happened to me was when I was on the beach of Sandy Lane Hotel with my friend Andrew Neil. We lay on adjacent sun-loungers. In those days, although the beach was meant to be for residents only, a certain member of the management team would accept back-handers and see that people who were not guests got to use the beach. There was a Jewish family whose father was very short and had about four sons, one of whom was crippled. He was very nice but the others were noisy and brought ghetto blasters on to the beach. So I said to the beach attendant, "Will you please see that Mr X and his family are positioned some way away from me." The beach attendant obviously told this to Mr X and his family and, while Andrew Neil and I are lying on the beach, Mr X comes over and shouts in a very loud and common voice, "I wanna see you." Well, he could see me. I was there on a sun-lounger in front of him. I stood up thinking, "Well, where does he want to see me?" whereupon Mr X started a tirade, "I have been coming to this hotel longer than you have. How dare you say you don't want my family anywhere near you. I have a crippled son. It's a total disgrace. What I should do is take that beach umbrella and stick it up your arse. And then when I've stuck it up your arse, I'll open it!" At this point Andrew Neil looked up and said, "If I'd known it was going to be this much fun I wouldn't have brought a book." I thought that was all pretty funny.

When I went to Israel I took with me a number of movie stars for a film called *Appointment with Death*. One of them was Peter Ustinov, who everyone assumed was Jewish. In fact, he was extremely anti-Semitic with one side of his family white Russian and the other side Palestinian. At the movie press conference in Tel Aviv, a local journalist said, "Mr Ustinov, are you Jewish?" to which he replied very gruffly, "No, I'm not." The journalist pursued the matter and said, "Well, we always thought you were." To which Peter said, "Well, you're wrong." Also on the movie was Lauren Bacall, who had a really very Jewish name and was very pro-Jewish. The cast were in a room off a square in Jaffa and Peter was going on and on. Finally Bacall screamed at him, "Peter, you are a dreadful anti-Semite!" and walked out of the room, followed by the rest of the cast. Peter loves telling stories and suddenly his audience was gone so he came out of the square and started telling stories to a Jewish attendant who was sweeping the square. Another time we were in a Chinese restaurant and Peter went to the only other two people in the room and started telling them stories. His stories, I might add, were extremely amusing and he was of course a wonderful mimic. In spite of being a bit of a monster – he never remembered his lines – I liked him. Towards the end of the movie we were dining in Haifa and Peter said to me, "If you were living in Israel, Michael, where would you like to live?" Now I actually enjoyed Israel very much to my surprise but I answered, "By the airport, Peter, so I can get out easily." To which Ustinov said, "I wish I could come out with remarks like that." I said, "Well you can't, Peter, because you're a well-known anti-Semite and they don't sound as good coming from you."

He was a dear friend, Peter, until the day he died, and he was responsible for the finest after-dinner speech I've ever heard in my life. Sometime after the movie, I got the Directors' Guild of Great Britain to give a Lifetime Achievement Award to Stanley Kubrick, who unfortunately died a couple of weeks before the ceremony. But all Stanley's family turned up. I hadn't seen Peter for a long time and when I did it was a shock. He'd become a very old man, fumbled, shuffled, he didn't look as if he'd last the evening. When the time came for him to make his speech – and he'd been chosen because he was in *Spartacus* directed by Stanley Kubrick – he came slowly on to the stage. The minute he got behind the microphone there was a transformation. Like all true professionals, something kicked in and he was no longer at death's door. He was the old witty Peter Ustinov in full flood. He proceeded to give a detailed account of the first script reading of *Spartacus*. He imitated exactly what everybody said and how they said it. I'm talking here about Kirk Douglas, Laurence Olivier, John Gavin and all the others. It was a stunningly brilliant speech and unquestionably the funniest I've ever heard. When it finished he suddenly became an old man again and shuffled back to my table where he sat comatose for the rest of the evening.

So humour can be a great pick-me-up. It can restore life to the almost dead. In 1963, I produced a theatre show at the Comedy Theatre called *Nights at the Comedy*. It was a sort of variety show hosted by a man called Daniel Farson. When I say I produced it, I was junior producer to a very peculiar gentleman called William Donaldson. During the first week of the run, William Donaldson ran out of money and vanished. This left the cast unpaid and in the lurch. There was, and rightly so, some considerable fury backstage. There were many distinguished artists involved. It was the first show ever done in the West End by Jimmy Tarbuck and also included a very famous old comedian called Jimmy James. Along with them, various other people were now denuded of their salary. I went round the dressing rooms to try and appease people, which of course I could not, and the one who took it very well was Jimmy James. He said, "Michael, I've been in the business over fifty years, I've seen this happen many times. Don't upset yourself about it."

Some humour is in such bad taste that I come out with a remark and think, "My goodness, I've gone too far this time!" Such an event occurred when I was making a movie called *Hannibal Brooks*. I came back to England every weekend to see the rushes and then returned to Austria. On this particular occasion I returned to Austria to be told that one English stuntman, who was very gung-ho but not too bright, had driven a German World War II vehicle into a crowd of people. "He hit a young man," I was told, and broke his leg and arm. "Oh well," I said, "that's one back for the six million." A visiting journalist came down the next day, was told of this remark and printed it in a London evening paper. I was expecting to get heavily criticised. Instead I've never had so many letters of congratulations and compliments for anything I ever said!

Moishe Pipick is a wonderful phrase used by Jews. Moishe Pipick is, as it were, the lowest of the low. When the highly mercurial film producer Menahem Golan had sold some movies to Warner Brothers but could not deliver them because he'd sold them to somebody else as well, I said, "Menahem, will Warner Brothers not take you to court to get the money back?" He said, "No, they won't. The worst they can do is call me Moishe Pipick."

There are people who collect jokes. They insist on telling you jokes on the telephone. And when you meet them over a dinner they tell non-stop jokes that are so dirty and so horrible that nobody wants to hear them. In this case I'm thinking of a very distinguished British actor whose wife continually upbraids him to stop telling these stupid jokes, as indeed do I. There's also a well-known rock musician. They are both very nice people but they seem to have this absolutely insatiable desire to tell endless dirty jokes, each one more vulgar and less funny than the one before. The only thing to do is try and shut them up, because it has nothing to do with humour but more to do with seeing how dirty the jokes can get before shocking people.

Funny remarks are rare. I recall one made by a

nurse who was visiting me in hospital with my wife Geraldine. I was in the Cromwell Hospital for a few days and I said on Friday evening, "How do I get out of here?" meaning who's going to release me officially from the hospital. So I said, "How do I get out of here?" to which Nurse Amparo replied, "Follow the exit signs." I thought that was very funny, but maybe that's because I'd recently come out of illness.

Of course there are things that are funny to me which are not funny to anybody else. The first time I ever directed anybody was on a raised ledge of a windowsill at my school. The actors, who were children, included a boy called Robert Brindley. He was meant to come on and do some acting. I hit out at the curtain where he was hiding behind and said, "Come on, Robert, you're on." But I pushed him out the window. We were one floor up. He fell to the ground and went around for the next two weeks with his arm in a sling. I obviously have a rather odd sense of humour because I found that extremely funny.

So now we come to Hymie. Hymie is the ever elusive wandering Jew. Things happen to him continually that do not happen to the rest of us but Hymie bears it all with good humour and skill. People say that such a person no longer exists. That's nonsense. I know lots of people who could be Hymie in attitude, appearance and marvellous sense of humour. So they unquestionably do exist. Hymie is the butt of jokes because they are things that happen to him in his real life. Our Hymie stories are either sent in by *Sunday Times* readers, or by friends, but they all have one thing in common: they're extremely funny. And here they are.

THE JOKES

Hymie is getting very excited about the publication of some new Jewish erotica... *50 Shades of Oy Vey*... Boom.

Mr Shapiro, the Matchmaker, goes to see Hymie who is, at the time, a confirmed bachelor. He says, "Hymie, don't leave it too late. I have exactly the girl you need. You only have to say the word and you'll meet and be married in no time." "Don't bother," replies Hymie, "I've two sisters at home who look after all my needs." "That's well and good," says the Matchmaker, "but all the sisters in the world cannot fill the role of a wife." "I said two sisters. I didn't say they were mine," responds Hymie.

Hymie and his wife Becky join their synagogue's Hebrew classes. At the end of their first week their teacher, Rabbi Goldbloom, asks Hymie, "So what do you think of my Hebrew class?" "It's not as bad as I thought it would be, Rabbi," Hymie replies. "Although if I'm honest," he adds, "I must admit that I really only have to learn the first part of every sentence." "Why's that?" asks Rabbi Goldbloom. "Because," says Hymie, "Becky always finishes my sentences for me."

Hymie is reading the paper. "Look at this," he says to Becky. "Police arrest two boys, one for drinking battery liquid, the other for smoking fireworks. They charged the first boy and let the other one off."

Hymie's friend Moishe goes to the doctor who tells him, "You're going to die." Moishe says, "I'd like a second opinion." The doctor says, "You're also very ugly."

Hymie asks Moishe, "How was the funeral?" Moishe replies, "All right but the music wasn't much good. We were the only two dancing."

Hymie is in Soho where he's approached by a lady of the night. "Would you sleep with me for £100?" she asks. "Well," says Hymie, "I'm not really tired but I could do with the money."

Hymie opens the door. A lovely girl says, "Your pal Moishe Pipick sent me as a present. I'm here to offer you super sex." Hymie replies, "I'll have the soup."

Hymie's friend Abe goes to confession. "I'm ninety-two years old, got a wife of seventy, children and grandchildren. Yesterday I picked up two college girls hitchhiking, went to a motel and had sex with each of them three times." The priest says, "Are you sorry for your sins?" Abe, "What sins?" Priest, "What kind of Catholic are you?" Abe, "I'm Jewish." Priest, "Then why are you telling me all this?" Abe, "I'm ninety-two years old, I'm telling everybody."

Hymie tells his friend Moishe, "I think I'm going to divorce my wife. She hasn't spoken to me in over two months." Moishe considers and says, "You'd better think it over, Hymie. Women like that are hard to find."

Becky, Hymie's wife, takes her duck to the vet. He says, "Sorry, it's dead." She says, "I don't believe it." The vet calls in a labrador dog. The dog sniffs the body of the duck, lowers its head dolefully, shakes it left to right and walks out. In comes a cat, licks the duck, lowers head, gives a sad nod of head and leaves. Vet says, "That'll be £1,000." Becky says, "That's outrageous." Vet responds, "It would have been £200 but you've got to add the lab report and the cat scan."

Hymie walks into the Ivy carrying a duck. The mâitre d' asks, "What are you doing with the pig?" Hymie replies, "You complete idiot, it's a duck." The mâitre d' says, "I was talking to the duck."

Hymie's friend Moishe says he is sleeping with a fabulous blonde – one of twins. Then he says he is also sleeping with the other twin. "How do you tell them apart?" Hymie asks. "Easy," he replies. "Her brother's got a moustache."

Hymie says, "I was reading a book about glue. Couldn't put it down."

Hymie asks, "How do you get a bear out of a tree with cheese? Camembert."

Hymie asks, "How do you turn a dishwasher into a snowmobile? Give her a shovel."

Hymie goes to the doctor, says, "I think I'm a moth." Doctor advises, "You should see a psychiatrist." Hymie says, "I was going to but your light was on."

Becky is caught shoplifting. The judge intones, "You stole a packet of twelve asparagus sticks, so I sentence you to twelve days in jail." Her husband, Hymie, says, "Excuse me, m'lud, she also stole two packs of peas."

A bank robber shoots the cashier and two customers who'd seen his face. "Did anyone else see my face?" he shouts. Hymie, in a timid voice, says, "I think my missus caught a glimpse."

Hymie is in the desert standing behind trestle tables, selling ties. A Taliban staggers up and says, "You Jewish bastard, I should shoot you. But I need water." Hymie says, "Water I don't do. I do ties, silk, wool. Here's a nice one – blue with white spots." The Taliban says, "Gimme water, you pig." Hymie says, "You want water, go over that sand dune there. Turn left. Walk a mile, take a right, go over two more sand dunes. There you'll find a restaurant. It does water." The Taliban lurches off, returns two hours later, parched, tongue cracked, in a terrible state. "I'll have the blue one with white spots," he says. "I should slit your throat. I get to the restaurant and your putz of a brother says he won't let me in without a tie."

Becky goes to a fortune teller. She's told, "Your husband is going to be beaten, mutilated and murdered." Becky asks, "Was I acquitted?"

Hymie is on safari. He wanders from the group and comes across a distressed young bull elephant with one leg in the air. Hymie approaches cautiously and finds a large piece of wood embedded in the elephant's foot. Hymie takes out his Swiss Army knife and carefully prises the wood out. The elephant raises and lowers his leg, looks lovingly at Hymie, extends his trunk and kisses him on the cheek, then walks away. Twenty years later Hymie is at the Chicago zoo. A large bull elephant stares at Hymie. It lifts its leg up and down, trumpets loudly and extends its trunk as if to kiss him. It's a magical moment. Hymie summons his courage and walks into the enclosure. He goes up to the elephant, which twirls its trunk around Hymie, slams him against the wall and kills him. Probably wasn't the same elephant.

Hymie says to Moishe, "We've been friends for years. I'd do anything for you. If I had two houses I'd give you one." "That's very kind," says Moishe. "No problem," says Hymie, "if I had two cars, I'd give you one." "What if you had two chickens?" asks Moishe. "You putz," says Hymie. "You know I've got two chickens."

One winter, while skiing in the Alps, Hymie leaves the hotel at 8am and does not return by 5pm. The alarmed manager alerts the Red Cross. They search the slopes, eventually spotting a solitary figure skiing down an adjacent mountain. They call out, "Are you Hymie?" A voice replies, "Yes, who are you?" The team leader responds, "The Red Cross." Hymie yells, "I gave already!"

Two Jewish women are sitting quietly together, minding their own business.

Hymie is sitting on a bench; looks terrible – dishevelled, sloppy, depressed. The Rabbi says, "Hymie, pull yourself together. I'm going away for three weeks. Go out and meet people, get a hobby – a hobby would be good." The Rabbi returns. Hymie's a changed man: bright, smart, happy – totally different demeanour. The Rabbi says, "You look great, Hymie." Hymie responds, "I owe it to you, Rabbi. I did as you said: I got myself a hobby." The Rabbi asks, "What hobby?" Hymie replies, "Bees. I keep bees. I'm a beekeeper." The Rabbi exclaims, "But you've only got a one-room apartment – how do you keep bees?" Hymie produces a matchbox from his pocket. "I keep them in this box," he explains. The Rabbi says, "You can't keep bees in a box like that. They'll die." Hymie says, "Sure they did. Fuck 'em."

Hymie specials

What do you call a woman who knows where her husband is every night? A widow.

Hymie jokes, "No matter how much you push the envelope, it'll still be stationery."

Two silkworms have a race. They end up in a tie.

A grenade thrown into a French kitchen would result in Linoleum Blownapart.

A dog gives birth to puppies near the road and is cited for littering.

Atheism is a non-prophet organisation.

Becky, the seamstress, is walking home at night. A flasher opens his coat, revealing all. Becky says, "You call that a lining?"

Hymie announces, "The Irish SAS stormed Dublin zoo. Killed five gorillas, saved three ostriches."

Hymie tells Becky, "I've got a new aftershave called Crumbs. The birds love it."

Hymie is asked by a restaurant receptionist, "Do you have a reservation?" Hymie replies, "Do I look like a Red Indian?"

Hymie's US cousin Abe asks an Australian tour guide, "You're fourteen hours ahead of us?" "That's right," replies the tour guide. "So why did you not warn us of 9/11 then?" demands Abe.

Hymie is selling pretzels outside Stratford Tube station. Abe, a rich local, gives him £4, declines the bag of pretzels, and says, "It's for you." Every day for three years Abe gives Hymie £4 but never takes the pretzels. One day he gives £4 and Hymie says, "£7 now." "How come?" asks Abe. "The price of pretzels has gone up," says Hymie.

Hymie says, "I'm leaving England to live in Israel." His friend Abe asks, "What will you do there?" Hymie says, "I'm going to make cheese. I'll be a cheesemaker." "Make cheese?" says Abe. "What will you call it?" "I thought Cheeses of Nazareth would be a good name," replies Hymie.

Becky goes to buy a parrot. The shopkeeper says, "These two parrots are £300 each; this one's £30." Becky says, "What's wrong with the £30 parrot? Is he ill?" The shopkeeper says, "Nothing's wrong, but it's been working in a brothel." Becky says, "Brothel, shmothel: I'll have the £30 parrot, save £270." She takes the parrot home to her lovely house in Hampstead. The parrot says, "Fuck me! Another brothel." Becky's two daughters return from shopping. The parrot says, "Fuck me! Two more prostitutes." Then Becky's husband, Hymie, comes in from work. The parrot shouts, "Fuck me, Hymie! Haven't seen you for two weeks."

Hymie goes into a bank at Heathrow, says he's going to the south of France for two weeks, can he borrow £5,000? He'll leave his £230,000 Bentley as collateral. Hymie leaves the car in the bank's underground car park. Two weeks later he returns to collect it and pays back the £5,000 plus £6.58 interest. The bank manager has checked and now knows Hymie is a millionaire. "Why did you need to borrow £5,000, Mr Cohen?" he asks. Hymie shrugs and says, "Where else at Heathrow can I park for £6.58?"

Hymie jokes for you

"I thought I saw an eye doctor on an Alaskan island but it turned out to be an optical Aleutian."

When cannibals ate a missionary they got a taste of religion.

A hole has been found in a nudist camp wall. The police are looking into it.

Two hats were hanging on a hat rack. One said to the other, "You stay here, I'll go on a head."

A vulture boards an aeroplane carrying two dead racoons. The stewardess says, "I'm sorry, sir, only one carrion allowed per passenger."

Hymie says to his friend Moishe, "I have a little cash flow problem, can you lend me £100?" Moishe says, "But Hymie, two months ago I gave you £100, the month before that it was £200, and last year I lent you £1,000." Hymie replies, "Sure, sure, Moishe, but what have you done for me lately?"

Overheard at the London Olympics...
Hymie to a competitor: "Are you a pole vaulter?"
Competitor: "No, I'm German, but how do you know my name?"

Hymie calls over the waiter. "Are you sure you're the waiter I gave my order to?" he asks. "Yes, why do you ask?" replies the waiter. "Because I was expecting a much older man by now," says Hymie.

Hymie says, "Saw an AA man crying his eyes out. He was on his way to a breakdown."

Hymie says, "Definition of a juniper – an Israeli youth."

Hymie goes to Moishe's funeral. There's a new Rabbi, who never knew Moishe. He says, "Moishe was a wonderful man." "He was horrible," shouts Hymie from the back row. "Moishe was a great family man," says the Rabbi. "Rubbish," barks Hymie. "His family hated him." "Moishe gave tirelessly to charity," intones the Rabbi. "Never gave a penny to anyone," says Hymie. The Rabbi stops. "I'm not going on until one of you tells me something good about Moishe," he announces. Hymie yells, "His brother was worse."

Hymie says to his mother, "I've met a girl." "Oy vey," sighs Mama. So Hymie brings home three beautiful girls and asks his mother to guess which girl he's fallen in love with. "The one in the middle," she says. "How did you know, Mama?" asks Hymie. "I didn't like her," she answers.

Hymie looks in Abe's fridge and sees an empty milk bottle. "Why do you keep an empty milk bottle in the fridge, Abe?" he asks. Abe replies, "That's in case someone wants black coffee."

Hymie meets Mrs Cohen in the street. "No? What's going on?" he asks. "Vell," says Mrs Cohen, "I've got good news and bad news." "What's bad?" asks Hymie. "My son Jacob, he just told us he's gay. My boy, suddenly he's gay." "That's not serious," says Hymie. "Lots of talented people are gay. Nothing to worry about. What's the good news?" "He's marrying a doctor," says Mrs Cohen.

There are two gates to heaven. One has a sign, 'For husbands who are henpecked'; the other, 'Husbands who have *not* been henpecked'. In front of this gate, all by himself, is Hymie. A passing angel asks, "Are you certain you're waiting in the right place?" "I'm not sure," replies Hymie. "My wife told me to stand here."

Hymie has a kosher restaurant. His friend Abe comes in. A Chinese waiter goes over. Abe orders and speaks to the Chinese waiter, who responds in Yiddish. When the waiter goes, Abe says to Hymie, "Unbelievable. Only you could find a Chinese waiter you could teach to speak perfect Yiddish." Hymie says, "Not so loud. He thinks it's English."

Hymie's in a restaurant, head bent, his ear close to his fish. The waiter notices this. "I'm talking with the fish," explains Hymie. "What does he say?" asks the waiter. "He tells me he's from the River Dee in Scotland," replies Hymie. "So how are things in the Dee now?" asks the waiter. "He doesn't know," replies Hymie. "It's been so long since he was there."

Weinberg is driving his convertible Ferrari down a Mayfair street. At the traffic lights, a Rolls-Royce Corniche Convertible draws up next to him. Weinberg calls out, "Steinberg, it's me, Weinberg. We were at school together. For fifty years we've not seen each other." Steinberg replies, "What a coincidence, let's celebrate, go to the Ritz, have a slap-up lunch." At that moment a beaten-up Skoda stops alongside them. Steinberg says in amazement, "Look, it's Hymie Cohen. He was in our class too." He calls out, "Hey, Hymie. It's Weinberg and Steinberg. Your old schoolmates. Remember us?" Hymie says, "Wonderful to see you." "Hymie," says Weinberg, "We're going to the Ritz for lunch. You come with us." Hymie responds,

"You fellows are obviously doing very well. I'm not doing so good. I can't afford the Ritz." "Never mind, come," says Steinberg. "Don't eat."

Hymie is taking an afternoon nap. His wife, Becky, comes in from her bridge lunch. Hymie opens one eye and asks, "How was it, dear?" Becky replies, "Do you want the good news or the bad news?" Hymie says, "In my state of health, what's the good news?" "The airbags on the new Rolls-Royce work perfectly," says Becky.

Hymie and a friend walk into a bar. You'd have thought his friend would have seen it and ducked.

Hymie is driving along a country road and sees a sign: '1 mile to Abe's Café & Talking Dog.' Hymie goes in and says to Abe, "Where's the talking dog?" Abe replies, "At the back." Hymie goes round. Lying there is an old dog. "Are you the talking dog?" Hymie asks. The dog says, "Sure I am." Hymie is stunned. "You can really talk," he says. "How did you learn?" The dog says, "I used to work for the Metropolitan Police. They taught me to talk. Criminals spoke in front of me. They thought I was just a dog. I did so well I was seconded to the CIA. They taught me Russian and sent me to Moscow; then I learnt Chinese and went to Beijing. I got tired of being a spy so I joined the British embassy in Paris, later in Rome. But now I have a family, I've retired." Hymie goes back to Abe. "That's incredible," he says. "Your dog can really talk. Would you sell him?" "Sure," says Abe. "How much?" asks Hymie. "£10," replies Abe. "Only £10 for a talking dog?" exclaims Hymie. "Aw, the dog's full of crap," says Abe. "He never did any of the things he told you about."

Hymie is having dinner at the Ivy with his wife, Becky. A young girl comes to the table and makes a big fuss of Hymie. When she leaves, Becky asks, "Who was that?" "That," says Hymie, "was my mistress." Becky is furious. "Our marriage is over," she says. "I want a divorce. Tomorrow I go to the solicitor." "Becky," says Hymie. "If you get a divorce you'll have no more shopping at Prada, no driving round in the Rolls, no south of France..." He tails off as their friend, Abe, enters and waves at them. He's with a young girl. "Who's that with Abe?" asks Becky. "That's his mistress," replies Hymie. Becky thinks for a moment, then says, "Ours is better."

Mrs Cohen gets a new flat. She phones her friend Becky and says, "Becky, you have got to see this apartment – balconies, views over the parks. Listen, you go to Regent's Park Tube. When you come out, Becky, take a left. A few yards down on your right you'll see Farley Court. Ring the doorbell with your right elbow. Push the door with your left elbow. Then you're in a lobby. On your left is a list of apartments – push No. 12 with your left elbow. You'll hear a buzz. Push the glass doors with your right elbow. In the hall facing you is the lift – press the call button with your right elbow. When you enter the lift, push Floor 3 with your left elbow. When the lift stops, push the door open with your right elbow. Ahead of you is my flat – No. 12. Push the bell with your left elbow. I'll come and greet you." Becky says, "What's all this with the elbows? Left elbow, right elbow – what are you talking about?" "Well," says Mrs Cohen, "you're not coming empty-handed, Becky, are you?"

Hymie gets a new job as an announcer on Radio 4. He says, "Good morning, this is Radio 4 on 94.6 megahertz. To you, 90 megahertz."

Hymie wins £20m on the lottery. His wife, Becky, asks, "What shall we do about the begging letters?" Hymie says, "Keep sending them out."

Hymie is driving his new BMW convertible down a country lane. As he approaches a bend in the road, a car comes round the corner in front of him and the lady driver shouts out, "Pig!" Which, for a good Jewish boy, is probably the lowest insult. Quick as a flash, Hymie responds with the worst thing he can, "Woman driver!" Then he turns the bend in the road and hits the pig.

Hymie is on holiday in Israel when his wife, Becky, suddenly has a heart attack and dies. The Israeli undertaker says, "I can bury her here for £1,500 or I can fly her to England and my associate firm will bury her. That, including the flight, will cost £6,000." Hymie thinks for a minute. "Just have her shipped home," he says. The undertaker asks, "Why spend extra money when Becky can be buried in the Jewish homeland for so much less?" Hymie replies, "Long ago a man died and was buried here. Three days later he rose from the dead. I just can't take that chance."

Hymie decides its time his son Jacob got married. So he and his wife, Becky, call in the shotchen. A shotchen is a Jewish lady who makes introductions with a view to marriage. "I vant you to find for my boy Jacob the most marvellous example of Jewish womanhood," explains Hymie. The shotchen goes off and returns three weeks later. "Have I got a girl for your Jacob," she announces. "This girl runs a kosher house, she goes to a synagogue three times a week; not only that, she knows all the prayers by heart. This girl is the perfect example of Jewish womanhood at its finest. And on top of all that, not only is this girl a lovely person, she is a real beauty. She's beautiful." Jacob says, "Excuse me, could I ask you something?" "Sure," says the shotchen. "Is she good in bed?" asks Jacob. "Vell," replies the shotchen. "Some say yes, some say no."

Hymie tells the doctor he's worried about his poor sex life with his wife. Dr Smith examines him and finds nothing wrong. He says, "There's an easy solution, Hymie, just run ten miles every day for seven days. Let me know how you get on." A week later, Hymie phones Dr Smith. "Well?" asks the doctor. "Did it work?" "How should I know?" said Hymie. "I'm seventy miles from home."

Hymie is feeling unwell. The doctor examines him and tells Hymie he has only two weeks left to live. Hymie says, "In that case I'll have the first week in July and the last week in November."

Hymie is having coffee with his friend, Jacob. Jacob says, "Hymie, do you remember Moishe Pipick?" Hymie answers, "Sure, I know Moishe well." Jacob asks, "And Abe Schwanz?" Hymie says, "Abe, lovely man, known him for years." Jacob says, "Vell, a terrible thing happened. Moishe came home last night and found his wife in bed with Abe Schwanz. He took a gun and shot Abe dead, then turned the gun on himself." "That's awful," says Hymie. "Mind you, could have been worse." "How could it have been worse?" asks Jacob. Hymie replies, "If it had happened the night before, I'd be dead now."

Hymie goes to the doctor, says, "Nobody listens to me." The doctor shouts out, "Next!"

The doctor calls Hymie and says, "Your cheque came back." Hymie responds, "So did my arthritis."

Hymie is driving his new Rolls-Royce down Golders Green high street. He sees an old friend, lowers the window and shouts: "Abe, how are you?" Abe says, "Not so good. Don't even have anywhere to sleep. Could you give me £10 for a bed?" Hymie says, "Bring it in tomorrow, I'll let you know."

Hymie rents a remote Highland cottage to go and consider life. After a couple of days, there's a knock on the door. Hymie opens it and sees a tall, athletic Highlander, who says, "We saw you were alone

– we'd like to ask you to a ceilidh." Hymie asks, "What's a ceilidh?" The Highlander explains, "It's a Scottish party. We start with drinks, and then dinner, followed by dancing. After that we have some sex." Hymie says, "Sounds nice to me. What should I wear?" "Doesn't matter," replies the Highlander. "It's only you and me."

Hymie is dying. At the bedside are his wife, Becky, and their four sons. Three of them are of medium height with dark hair but the oldest, Maurice, is 6ft tall with blond hair. Hymie gasps, "Tell me the truth, Becky. Our oldest boy, Maurice – am I really his father?" Becky says, "Of course you are, Hymie." Hymie mutters, "Swear that on your life, Becky." Becky replies, "I swear on my life, Hymie, that Maurice is your son." Hymie smiles and dies. Becky looks up. "Thank God he didn't ask me about the other three," she says.

Hymie is dying, his wife, Becky, at his bedside. In a whisper Hymie says, "I have to make a confession, Becky." Becky says, "Don't talk – you need to rest." Hymie persists, "I must die in peace, Becky. I slept with your sister and your best friend. There, I've got it off my chest." "I know, darling," says Becky. "Now be quiet and let the poison work."

A policeman comes to Hymie's front door holding a photo of his mother-in-law. "Do you know this woman?" he asks. "Yes," replies Hymie. The policeman says, "I'm afraid it looks as if she's been hit by a bus." "I know," says Hymie, "but she has a lovely personality."

Hymie is on his deathbed. He says to his wife, "Becky, when we lived in the village in Russia and there was a pogrom, you were with me." "Of course," says Becky. Hymie continues, "Then we moved to Moscow, where I became a tailor and the shop went bust. You, Becky, were with me." "Of course I was," says Becky. "When we came to England, Becky, and my shoe business failed, you were with me, by my side," says Hymie. "I'll always be with you, Hymie. You can rely on me. I love you," says Becky. "And now," says Hymie, "I'm dying and here you are, holding my hand, still with me." "You can always count on me," says Becky, adoringly. "You know what, Becky?" whispers Hymie. "You're a fucking jinx."

Rachel's dog jumps in a lake, gets into trouble and begins to drown. Hymie, passing by, dives in and saves it. He gives the dog to Rachel. "He'll be fine," says Hymie. "Are you a vet?" she asks. "Vet?" says Hymie, "I'm bloody soaking."

Hymie is recently widowed. After a respectful time of mourning, Hymie, now old and lonely, ventures out to the local pub. There he meets a lady who invites him back to her place for a nightcap. Once in her house, they start to get friendly. She says, "Would you like to go upstairs and have sex?" Hymie replies, "I can't do both."

Hymie comes home early one afternoon to find his wife, Becky, lying naked on their bed. "Why are you naked?" asks Hymie. "Because I haven't got a thing to wear," replies Becky. "Nonsense!" cries Hymie, throwing open the wardrobe door. "You've got this white dress here and this blue one – oh, hello, Izzie – and this green one."

The secretary of a golf club approaches the 10th green after complaints. Three men are shouting obscenities over the prostrate body of a fourth man.

"What's going on?" asks the secretary. A golfer replies, "This is a serious game. We're playing for £100 a hole. My partner has just had a stroke and Hymie wants to count it."

Hymie's taking a weekend at his house in Norfolk. He hears a shot. A duck falls onto his potting shed roof and rolls off into his back yard. Hymie goes to get it, when a large hunter appears and says, "Leave that, it's mine." Hymie replies, "It hit my shed and fell in my yard. So it's my duck." The hunter says, "Don't be dumb. I've been shooting for two days – that's the first thing I got. I want it." Hymie says, "OK, this is what we'll do. I'll kick you in the groin, then you kick me in the groin. Last man standing gets the duck." So, Hymie goes back a few paces, takes a run and swings an enormous kick at the hunter's groin. The hunter screams in pain and rolls on the ground in agony. After ten minutes the hunter gets up and says, "Now it's my turn to kick you in the groin." Hymie says, "Forget it. You can have the duck."

Hymie raises enough money to send his Rabbi to Hawaii for a week. When the Rabbi walks into his hotel room there's a beautiful naked woman lying on the bed. She greets the Rabbi with, "Hi, Rabbi, I'm a little extra Hymie arranged for you." The Rabbi is furious. He rings Hymie in Golders Green and shouts, "Where is your respect? I'm the moral leader of our community. You've not heard the end of this." He slams the phone down. The naked woman starts to get dressed. The Rabbi says, "Where are you going? I'm not angry with you."

Hymie's grandson comes home from school and says proudly, "Grandpa, I've got a part in my school play." "What part is it?" asks Hymie. The boy replies, "I'm playing a Jewish husband." Hymie responds, "Go back and tell your teacher you want a speaking part."

Two beggars sit near the Vatican. One holds a cross, the other the Star of David. Passers-by put money into the hat of the man with the cross, but give none to the beggar with the Star of David. A priest comes over and says, "I've been watching you two. You can't expect people here to give money to a man holding a Star of David. In fact, they probably give more money to the man with the cross out of spite."

The beggar with the Star of David turns to the one with the cross and says, "Hymie, look who's trying to teach the Cohen brothers about marketing."

Hymie's out and his wife Becky answers the phone. "Hello-ah," she says. A man responds, "You're pent up and frustrated. You want me to come over, throw you on the bed, rip your clothes off, make love to you and give you an experience such as you've never known." Becky says, "All this you can tell from Hello-ah?"

Hymie tells his friend Moishe, "A man is incomplete until he is married. Then he's truly finished."

Hymie decides to give a dinner party. To impress his north London friends he hires a butler. He says to his wife, Becky, "How many people should we have?" "Eight guests is enough," replies Becky, "so there'll be ten of us." Becky is out having her hair done when Hymie comes home from work. He sees the table is laid for twelve people. "Why did you lay the table for twelve?" he asks the butler. "We told you ten only." The butler replies, "It's all right, sir, Mrs Isaacs phoned to say she's bringing the Bagels."

Hymie goes to the doctor. After he leaves the surgery, the doctor calls in his wife, Becky. "Hymie has phenomenally high blood pressure," he explains. "If he carries on like this, he'll be dead in a month. But you can prevent it. Prepare him a fresh healthy meal every day, don't let Hymie lift a finger around the house and, most importantly, make love to him five times a week. Do that and he'll make a full recovery." On the way home, Hymie asks Becky, "What did the doctor say to you?" Becky replies, "He said you're going to die."

Hymie, sitting next to a Muslim on a plane, has just been served a whisky. The stewardess asks the Muslim if he'd like a drink. He replies in disgust, "I'd rather be raped by a dozen whores than let liquor pass my lips." Hymie hands his drink back and says, "Me too. I didn't know we had a choice."

Hymie is on the phone to his friend, Abe. Suddenly the line to Abe is lost. Hymie phones the operator to complain. He says, "Operator, I was in mid conversation with someone, they've vanished. What's going on?" The operator says, "Well, you were cut off." Hymie says, "I know. That happened when I was a baby. But it hasn't affected my hearing before."

Hymie is suffering from stress. The doctor says to him, "I could give you pills, but I'll give you advice. When I feel stressed I go home and make passionate love to my wife. Try that." Two weeks later he calls Hymie to ask how he's getting on. "Fine," says Hymie. "I did as you suggested, I feel much more relaxed. And by the way, that's a really nice house you've got."

Becky is cooking Sunday lunch. She says to her husband, Hymie, "Go to the garden and dig up a large cabbage." Hymie is bending over the cabbage when he has a massive heart attack and dies. That afternoon Becky's friend, Sadie, comes round and is told the story. "That's terrible," says Sadie. "What did you do?" "What could I do?" replies Becky. "I opened a tin of peas instead."

Hymie says to his wife, Becky, "I'm giving you a very special birthday present. I've reserved the best graveyard plot in Golders Green cemetery, right under that wonderful chestnut tree, just for you." Becky is not amused. The next year she gets nothing. She says to Hymie, "So where's my birthday present?" Hymie replies, "Why should I give you a birthday present? You never used the one I gave you last year."

Hymie is sitting in a café, muttering, "Eighty-nine times, eighty-nine times but never again." His friend Moishe comes in and overhears this. "What's up, old friend?" asks Moishe. "Eighty-nine times I invited Michael Winner to dinner. Eighty-nine times," says Hymie. "You've given dinner to Michael Winner eighty-nine times?" says Moishe. "That's very generous of you." "No," explains Hymie. "Eighty-nine times I invite him." "Then what's wrong?" asks Moishe. "Last week he turned up," says Hymie. "Never again."

Hymie's wife, Becky, is flying in a small propeller plane, just her sitting next to the pilot. The pilot suddenly has a heart attack. Becky calls into the radio, "Mayday! Mayday! Help me. My pilot had a heart attack. He's dead. I don't know how to fly." A calming voice comes on the radio, saying, "This is air traffic control. Your message has been received. I'll talk you through it – I've a lot of experience with this problem. Firstly give me your current height and position." Becky says, "I'm 5ft 4in. and I'm in the front seat." "OK," says the voice from the tower, "repeat after me: Our Father, who art in heaven..."

Hymie gets sent to a firing squad with a Frenchman and an Englishman. They're granted one last meal. The Frenchman asks for foie gras and snails, and is served the finest of both. The Englishman requests a Sunday roast: he gets the best beef, Yorkshire pudding, the lot. Hymie says, "Just give me a bowl of strawberries." "Strawberries?" replies the guard. "They're out of season." "So?" says Hymie, "I'll wait."

Hymie was bemoaning to his wife, Becky, that, as the years passed, a sense of emasculation was depressing him. "I can't even remember the last time you said you enjoyed sex," he said. Taking his hand gently, Becky responded, "Hymie, why would you remember? You weren't even there."

Hymie runs a delicatessen. A duck comes in and asks for a bowl of chicken soup and a salt beef sandwich. Hymie says, "But you're a duck." "So?" replies the duck. Hymie serves the duck and says, "I didn't mean to be rude, but we don't get many ducks in here." The duck explains, "I'm working in the block of flats down the road. I'm a plasterer, that's what I do, plastering." The duck comes in regularly. Then Hymie's friend Moishe, who has a circus, comes in. Hymie says, "Moishe, there's a duck who comes in here, speaks fluent English, has a bowl of soup and a salt beef sandwich." Moishe says, "I'll give him a job." The next day Hymie says to the duck,

"I've a great opportunity for you. My friend runs a circus. He wants to employ you." The duck asks, "A circus?" "Yes," says Hymie. The duck continues, "One of those places where animals are in cages, then they let them out to be part of a big show in a tent?" "Right," says Hymie. "And," the duck says, "at the top of the tent there's a hole to let the air out?" "Right," responds Hymie. The duck says, "What the fuck do they want with a plasterer?"

Hymie and Becky were on holiday in Devon. A balloon trip is available for £300. Hymie says, "It's too much." Finally, the pilot says, "I'll take you both up for nothing, on the condition you don't utter a sound when we're up." They went for an amazing ride. When the balloon landed, the pilot says to Hymie, "I did everything, spinning, oscillating, you never said a word." "True," says Hymie. "Even when Becky fell out I kept quiet."

Hymie says to Becky, "Have you heard? The Jewish religion and the Mormon religion have combined forces. Their headquarters are in Salt Beef City."

Hymie decides to bond with his son, so he takes him to the local pub. He buys two pints of real ale. His son doesn't like the taste so Hymie drinks both. He then buys two pints of Guinness. Same result. Finally he buys two large scotches. His son hates it, so Hymie has to drink both. By now, Hymie has had enough, so he puts his son back in the pram and takes him home.

Becky, Hymie's wife, is giving advice to her niece. "Ruthie," she says, "here are five tips for a woman looking to be married. 1) It's important that the man helps you around the house and has a job. 2) It's important the man makes you laugh. 3) It's important to find a man you can count on and who doesn't lie to you. 4) It's important that the man loves you and spoils you. 5) It's important that these four men don't know each other."

Hymie and Becky arrive at JFK airport and take a taxi to their hotel. The driver asks in a thick Bronx accent, "Where are you from?" Hymie replies, "London, England." Becky can't understand the driver's accent. "What did he say?" she asks. Hymie says, "He asked where we were from. I told him London, England." The driver asks, "Where in London?" "Just outside London," says Hymie. "A place called Stanmore." Becky asks, "What did he say now?" Hymie replies, "He asked what part of London. I explained just outside London, in Stanmore." The taxi driver says, "During the war I was stationed at the American air force base in Stanmore. I met a girl there and had the worst sex of my life." "What did he say?" asks Becky. Hymie replies, "He thinks he knows you."

Becky is extremely proud of her grandson, who has recently joined the army. She reads Hymie a letter from him. "How long did it take Montgomery to become a field marshal?" she asks. "About thirty years," replies Hymie. "Well," says Becky, "our Leon, he's only been in the army three weeks and already they've made him a court martial."

Hymie turns up at the local Ku Klux Klan meeting. "What are you doing here, Hymie Cohen?" asks the chief wizard. Hymie replies, "I was hoping to make an appointment with the linen buyer."

Hymie tells Moishe his wife Becky must be dead. "Why should you say such a thing?" asks Moishe. Hymie replies, "Well, the sex is the same. But the ironing's piling up."

When Hymie and Abe were forty-five they went to Ryan's for a meal because the waitresses all wore short skirts and plunging necklines. When they were fifty-five they went to Ryan's because the food and wine were good. At sixty-five they went to Ryan's because it had wheelchair access. And when they were eighty-five they went to Ryan's because they had never been there before.

Hymie is involved in a motorway pile-up. When he wakes in the hospital the doctor says, "You'll be fine, Mr Cohen, but sad to say your willy was chopped off in the wreck and we couldn't find it. You've got £9,000 insurance compensation. We can build you a new one for £1,000 an inch. You'd better discuss with your wife what size she'd prefer." Hymie agrees to consult his wife, Becky. The doctor comes back the next day and asks, "What's the decision?" Hymie replies, "We're having granite worktops."

Hymie goes into Victoria's Secret to purchase a negligee for his wife, Becky. He's shown various negligees; the more sheer they are, the higher the price. Hymie opts for the sheerest and pays £400. At home he presents it to Becky and asks her to go upstairs and model it for him. Becky thinks, "Oy vey! This is so sheer, I won't put it on. I'll model naked and then take it back tomorrow and get the £400." She appears naked on the balcony and strikes a pose. Hymie says, "Good grief! For £400 you'd think they'd at least have ironed it."

Hymie is pulled over by the police for driving at 25mph on the M25. "Why are you driving so slowly?" asks the policeman. Hymie replies, "Vell, it says M25. I thought that was the speed limit." The policeman says, "The road number is nothing to do with the speed limit." Then he notices Hymie's parents, Sarah and Issac, shaking in the back seat, looking terrified. "What's wrong with your passengers?" asks the policeman. "Don't worry, officer, they're fine," replies Hymie. "They're always a bit squeamish when we come off the A217."

Hymie is cleaning his new Volvo. Abe, passing by, says: "I see you got rid of the old banger, then." Hymie replies, "No, the wife's still with me."

Hymie says to his wife, Becky, "Tell me, darling, truthfully, how many men have you slept with?" Becky replies, "Only you, my precious. With all the others I was awake."

Abe meets Hymie and says, "You don't look so good. What happened?" "Vell," says Hymie, "Becky and I come across this fairy. She says, 'Anything you want, tell me, you'll get it.' Becky says, 'I'd like to go on a world cruise.' Flick of the wand, Becky's holding two £20,000 tickets for a world cruise. Then she says to me, 'Hymie, what about you?' I whispered, 'Madame Fairy, I'd like a wife thirty years younger than me.' Whoosh, goes the wand. Suddenly I'm eighty years old. No vonder I don't look so good."

A petrol station owner put up a sign: 'Free sex with fill-up.' Hymie pulls in, fills his tank and asks for his free sex. The owner tells him to pick a number from one to ten. "If you guess right, you'll get the sex." Hymie says, "Eight." The garage owner responded: "Close, but it was seven." A week later Hymie pulls in with his friend Abe for a fill-up. Again he asks for the free sex. This time Hymie guesses, "Two." The owner said, "Sorry, it was three." As they drove off Hymie said to Abe, "I think that game is rigged. He doesn't really give away free sex at all." Abe replied, "No, it's definitely genuine. My wife won twice last week."

Hymie decides to make a will. He calls out to his wife, Becky, who's washing up in the kitchen. "Darling," he announces, "I'm going to leave everything to you." "You always have," Becky replies.

Becky and Hymie are in bed. Hymie is falling asleep. Becky says, "When we were courting, you used to hold my hand." Hymie holds her hand for a second then tries to get back to sleep. Becky says, "And then you used to kiss me." Hymie gives her a peck on the cheek and tries to return to sleep. Becky says, "And then you used to bite my neck." Angrily, Hymie throws back the covers and gets out of bed. "Where are you going?" asks Becky. "To get my teeth," Hymie replies.

Hymie is driving down the motorway when his mobile rings. He hears his wife's voice urgently warning him: "Hymie, I've just heard on the news there's a car going the wrong way on the M25. Please be careful." "It's not just one car," replies Hymie, "it's hundreds of them."

Hymie's playing cards. His pal, Abe, bets £5,000, loses and dies of a heart attack. Hymie volunteers to break the sad news to his widow. His friends say he must be diplomatic. Hymie rings the bell, tells Abe's widow: "Your husband lost £5,000 at cards. He's too frightened to come home." "Tell him to drop dead," she responds. "Right," says Hymie.

Hymie goes to synagogue with a dog. The Rabbi says, "This is a house of worship. You can't bring a dog in here." "Whaddya mean?" asks Hymie. "This is a Jewish dog. See, he's got his skullcap (kippa) in a bag." He looks down at the dog. "Kippa," says Hymie. The dog opens the bag, takes out a skullcap and puts it on. "Tallit," says Hymie. The dog stands on its hind legs, takes out a prayer shawl and puts that on. "Daven," says Hymie. The dog starts to pray. "This is fantastic," says the Rabbi. "Incredible. Take him to Hollywood. Get him on TV, in the movies. He'll make millions of dollars." "You speak to him," says Hymie. "He wants to be a doctor."

Hymie's teenage daughter, Ruth, admits to her parents, "I'm pregnant." Becky screams, "What pig did this to you?" Ruth makes a phone call. Half an hour later a distinguished, grey-haired man wearing a skullcap steps out of his Mercedes. He sits with Hymie, Becky and Ruth. "I'm afraid I can't marry Ruth because of my family situation," he explains, "but I'll provide generously for your daughter for the rest of her life. If she gives birth to a girl, I'll bequeath her two retail furniture stores, a deli, a condo in South Beach and a million-dollar bank account. If she has a boy, I'll bequeath him a chain of jewellery stores and $25m. However, if there's a miscarriage, I'm not sure what to do." Becky places a hand on the man's shoulder and says, "Don't worry – you'll try again."

Hymie dies. Becky, heartbroken, goes to a medium, who puts her in touch with her beloved husband. "Are you happy, Hymie?" she asks. "Very happy," responds Hymie. "What do you do all day?" asks Becky. "I have salad for breakfast," explains Hymie. "Then I have sex all morning, a salad lunch, then sex all afternoon. Salad for dinner, then it's sex all night." "But Hymie," says Becky, "I thought heaven was a holy place." "Who said anything about heaven?" asks Hymie. "I'm a rabbit on the heath."

Hymie returns from a business trip to New York and finds his wife, Becky, has been unfaithful while he was away. "Who was it?" he yells at Becky, "was it that bastard Sam?" "No," replies Becky, "not Sam." "So was it Abe, that degenerate old man?" "No, it certainly wasn't him." "Then it must have been that simpleton Moishe." "No, it wasn't Moishe either," replies Becky. Hymie is now very angry. "What's the matter?" he cries out, "are none of my friends good enough for you?"

Hymie calls easyJet to book a flight. The operator asks, "How many people are flying with you?" Hymie replies, "I don't know! It's your fucking plane!"

Hymie and Moishe are reading headstones at a nearby cemetery. Hymie says, "Crikey! There's a bloke here who was 152!" Moishe asks, "What was his name?" Hymie replies, "Miles, from London!"

Hymie works hard at the office, spends two nights each week bowling and plays golf every Saturday. His wife, Becky, thinks he's pushing it a bit so for his birthday she takes him to a local strip club. The doorman at the club says, "Hi, Hymie, how are you doing?" Becky is puzzled and asks if he's been to the club before. "Oh no," says Hymie, "he's in my bowling league." When they are seated, a waitress asks Hymie if he'd like his usual and brings over a Budweiser. Becky is becoming increasingly uncomfortable. She says, "How did she know that you drank Budweiser?" Hymie says, "I recognised her.

She's the waitress from the golf club. I always have a Budweiser at the end of the first nine, honey." A stripper then comes over, throws her arms around Hymie and starts to rub herself all over him saying, "Hi, Hymie, want your usual table dance, big boy?" Hymie's wife, now furious, storms out of the club. Hymie follows and sees her get into a cab. Before she can slam the door he jumps in. Hymie tries desperately to explain how the stripper must have mistaken him for someone else, but Becky is having none of it. She's screaming at him at the top of her lungs, calling him every four-letter word in the book. The cab driver turns around and says, "Gee, Hymie, you picked up a real bitch this time."

Hymie has been married to Becky for three weeks. They are madly in love. One evening, around 7pm, Hymie says to Becky, "I'm just popping out for a couple of hours." Becky says, "Ver are you going?" Hymie says, "I'm just nipping down to the bar, I fancy a cold beer." At this, Becky throws open the refrigerator and says, "You vanna beer, Hymie? Look at this. I've got beers from Belgium, England, Australia, Germany and America, have your beer right here with me, Hymie. You don't have to go out." Hymie says, "You don't understand, Becky. In the bar I get my beer in an ice-cold glass goblet." Becky throws open the deep freeze, takes out a glass goblet that's so cold she can hardly hold it. She says, "You vant a beer in an iced goblet, Hymie? Here's an iced goblet. Drink your beer here." Hymie says, "You don't understand, Becky, in the bar there are these vonderful snacks. There are canapés laid out all down the bar and bits and pieces of food. It's vonderful." Becky says, "You vant canapés and snacks Hymie?" She throws open the oven door and says, "Look we've got hot snacks, we've got burgers, we've got pasties, we've got all sorts of hot snacks. On the other hand, Hymie, if you want cold snacks," she throws open another fridge, "here we've got smoked salmon canapés, we've got quail's egg canapés, we've got everything here, Hymie, you don't have to go out." Hymie says, "Becky, darling, I love you very much but you don't understand. In the bar there is a certain camaraderie. There is conversation. There is ribaldry. There is swearing..." Becky says, "You vant swearing, Hymie? I'll give you swearing you stupid arsehole, shit face, moron. You dickhead. I'll give you swearing. Now this is what you fucking do. You take the fucking beer from the fridge here. You drink it in my fucking ice-cold mug. You eat my fucking canapés, you moron. And you stay in this house, prick-o-Charlie. Do you get it? You want fucking swearing? You're getting it from me. Now shut up and get the rules straight. You fucking stay here until I tell you to go." And they lived happily ever after.

During the war, Hymie and Moishe have a plan to assassinate Hitler. They learn that he drives by a certain corner at noon each day, so they wait for him there with their guns well hidden. At exactly noon they are ready to shoot, but there is no sign of Hitler. Five minutes later, nothing. Another five minutes goes by, but no sign of Hitler. By twelve-fifteen they start to give up hope. "My goodness," says Hymie. "I hope nothing's happened to him!"

Hymie and Becky go to see a divorce lawyer. The lawyer is shocked. "Why now?" he asks. "You've been together all this time. Why have you waited so long?" Becky replies, "We wanted to wait until the children died!"

Hymie is experiencing his first romance. He proposes to his love and takes her to a city jeweller to buy the engagement ring. The jeweller produces a lovely ring – £40,000, he says. Hymie asks for a more expensive ring. The jeweller produces a fabulous ring at £70,000. Hymie says, "I will take that one. Here is my cheque. I will return next week when the cheque has been cleared." He returns the following week. The jeweller says, "There was only £25 in your account." Hymie says, "I know, but just let me tell you what a marvellous weekend I had with her."

A Jewish man is riding on the subway reading an Arab newspaper. A friend of his, who happens to be riding in the same subway car, notices this strange phenomenon. Very upset, he approaches the newspaper reader. "Hymie, have you lost your mind? Why are you reading an Arab newspaper?" Hymie replies, "I used to read the Jewish newspaper, but what did I find? Jews being persecuted, Israel being attacked, Jews disappearing through assimilation and intermarriage, Jews living in poverty. So I switched to the Arab newspaper. Now what do I find? Jews own all the banks, Jews control the media, Jews are all rich and powerful, Jews rule the world. The news is so much better."

A man ponders whether sex on the Sabbath is a sin. He asks a priest, who, after extensive research, informs him that sex is work and is therefore not permitted on a Sunday. Not happy with this, he goes to ask a minister who gives him the same reply. Still not happy he seeks out his friend Hymie, who sends him to the ultimate authority: a man of thousands of years of tradition and knowledge, the local Rabbi. The Rabbi ponders a few moments and declares that sex is definitely play. The man, delighted, asks how he can be so sure. The Rabbi replies, "If sex were work my wife would have the maid do it."

Hymie, the mortician, is preparing a body with the biggest penis he's ever seen. "I have to show this to my wife," he says. So he cuts it off and takes it home in a box. He gives it to Becky. "Take a look at that!" he says. Becky opens the box. "Oh my God!" she screams, "Schwartz is dead!"

Hymie, the doctor, is walking through the town one day, when he is approached by Sister Assumpta, the headmistress of the local convent school. "Doctor," she says. "Would you do me and the school a great favour by giving our senior girls an educational talk

on men and sex? You're a man of the world and you would have more credibility with my girls." Hymie thinks for a moment, then agrees to give the talk. When he gets home he tells Becky, his wife, that he had been asked to give the convent girls a talk. "On what?" asks Becky. Embarrassed, Hymie hesitates for a moment and then blurts out, "Sailing!" A couple of days later, Becky is in town and she meets Sister Assumpta. "Oh my," says the nun, "your husband gave a most wonderful talk to my girls two days ago. He was so knowledgeable." "Well, I'm very surprised at that," says Becky, "after all, he's only done it twice; the first time he got sick, the second time his hat blew off and he hasn't tried it since!"

Hymie's parrot, Mordechai, can speak and sing beautifully. On Rosh Hashanah he takes him to synagogue and makes a £100 bet with his old nemesis, Samuel, that Mordechai can conduct the closing prayer better than the synagogue's Cantor. When the big moment comes, though, Mordechai is silent and stares blankly. Hymie is outraged. He takes the parrot home and is about to put it in a pot when the bird finally speaks: "Schmuck! Think of the odds we'll get on Yom Kippur!"

Hymie asks the waiter, "Is your ice-cream pure?" Waiter says, "As pure as the girl of your dreams." Hymie replies, "I'll have the chocolate sauce."

Hymie rings his mother (yes – she's still around!), "Hello, Ma, how are you?" "I'm thin," she replies. "Thin? Why, are you sick?" asks Hymie. "No. I just didn't dare to eat anything in case you called and my mouth was full and I couldn't speak."

Hymie is at the checkout at the supermarket. "Would you like a bag for life?" the assistant at the till asks him. "I've got one," says Hymie, "she's waiting in the car."

Married for three months, Hymie gets a sex manual from the local bookshop. "Look, Becky," he says, "the manual says it increases the man's enjoyment when the woman moans." "All right, Hymie," says Becky. "You tell me when and I'll moan." When they next make love and Hymie is getting increasingly excited, Becky asks, "Do I moan now, Hymie?" "No, not yet," comes the answer. A little while later, she asks, "Do I moan now, Hymie?" "No, not just yet," says Hymie. A little later still, she asks, "Do I moan now, Hymie?" "Yes! Yes!" says Hymie. Becky slaps her forehead. "What a day I've had! First, the washing machine wouldn't start..."

Hymie and his wife are walking past a swanky new restaurant one night. His wife says, "Did you smell that food? It smelt incredible." Being the nice guy that he is, Hymie thinks, "Damn it, I'll treat her!" So he walks her past it again!

Becky is dying. Hymie and all the family are gathered around her bed. Hymie says to Becky, "I know you will be with us for only a short while but you have been a marvellous wife, mother and grandmother. Is there anything I can do for you in the time remaining?" A very weak voice from Becky replies, "Before I go, please buy me something retail."

Hymie has had a difficult day at work, so on his way home he buys some expensive delicacies from the deli and then drops into a swanky cocktail bar to unwind with a few drinks. He orders a highball and when it comes it is so delicious that Hymie exclaims, "This is the best highball I have ever had in my life!" Just to check that he is not kidding himself, he orders another, which is just as good, and so, as time goes by, he has four more. Finally he says to the bartender, "These have been the best highballs I have ever had, and to show my appreciation, not only will I give you a £5 tip but (reaching into his shopping bag) I also give you this," and he pushes a live lobster across the bar. "Well, thank you, sir," says the bartender, "can I take this home for dinner?" "Well," says Hymie, "as a matter of fact he's eaten already but I don't see why you can't take him out to see a movie."

What are the three words that Hymie does not want to hear when he is making love? "Honey, I'm home."

Hymie has driven into town for an important appointment and can't find a parking place. In desperation he looks to the heavens and says, "Dear God, find me a parking place and I won't miss synagogue for a whole year," upon which a car reverses out of a space right in front of him. Hymie says, "Forget it, God, I just found one."

Hymie's brother has been diagnosed with Alzheimer's and, when told, says, "I hope it doesn't run in the family because my brother has got it as well!"

Hymie's wife had a near-death experience today. Silly cow thought she could hoover while the football was on!

Hymie is crossing the road with Father Patrick when a speeding car causes them both to stumble. As they pick themselves up, Father Patrick crosses himself and says a quick prayer. To his surprise he sees that Hymie also crosses himself. "I didn't know that members of the Jewish faith crossed themselves," he says. "I'm not crossing myself," Hymie replies, "I'm checking – spectacles, testicles, wallet and watch!"

Hymie and Becky are flying to Australia for their fortieth anniversary. Suddenly, over the public address system the captain announces, "Ladies and gentlemen, I have some very bad news. Our engines have ceased functioning and we will attempt an emergency landing. Luckily I see an uncharted island below us and we should be able to land on the beach. However, the odds are that we may never be rescued and will have to live the rest of our lives on the island." The plane lands safely on the island and Hymie turns to his wife and says, "Did we pay our recent synagogue bill?" "No, sweetheart," she responds. "Did you remember to send the cheque to Jewish Care for the appeal this month? Did we pay our Kol Nidre charity pledge?" asks Hymie. "Forgive me, Hymie. I was so excited about our holiday I forgot to send all cheques," says Becky. Hymie grabs her and gives her the biggest hug and kiss in forty years. Becky pulls away, "So why did you kiss me?" Hymie answers, "They will find us!"

Hymie's son Zak is getting a lecture from his mother, Becky. "Smoking, drinking, out all night ruining your health, you should settle down with a nice homely Jewish girl. Your father NEVER smoked, NEVER touched a drop of alcohol and stayed home every night with me." "Mum! Dad was only forty-two when he dropped dead." "Yes, yes," sighed Becky, "but at least he dropped dead healthy."

Hymie's 10-year-old son Jacob is in trouble with his teacher at school. He made exactly the same mistakes in his exam paper as the boy he sits next to in class. The teacher suspects he copied his neighbour's answers. When asked to explain how he made exactly the same mistakes as his neighbour, Jacob replies, "It's because we have the same teacher."

Hymie and Abe decide to go on safari to Kenya. Suddenly this enormous animal jumps out of the bush onto Abe's back. "Hymie! Hymie!" screams Abe, "Get this thing off my back. What's this thing on my back?" Hymie shouts back, "How do I know what this thing on your back is? Do you think I'm a furrier?!"

Hymie's son is a successful businessman in New York and invites Hymie to stay. While there, Hymie has a suspected heart attack and the son, only concerned about his father's health and irrespective of cost, books Hymie into a private room in one of the best clinics in New York. Unfortunately, the son has to travel on business so, seeing that Hymie is well cared for, he promises to be back in one week. On his return the son goes to the clinic only to be told that Hymie has checked out of the clinic and taken himself off to the municipal hospital across the street. From the superb facility in the clinic the son goes to the chaos of the municipal hospital to find Hymie in a ward of twenty other people. He asks, "Father, why are you here? Did you not like the other place?" "No," replies Hymie, "the other place was superb." "Well, was the food not good enough?" asks his son. "The food was fantastic," replies Hymie. "Were the staff rude to you then?" asks the son. "Not at all," replies Hymie. "The staff were excellent." "So why are you here then?" asks the increasingly exasperated son. To which Hymie replies, "Here? Here I can complain."

Hymie gets into bed on his wedding night and proceeds to consummate the marriage but Becky swiftly stops him and demands £5. "£5?" screams Hymie. "You are my wife. Why should I pay £5?" Becky replies that her mother had always done this in her marriage as her duty was to the husband and family so this was the only way that she could have a little pin money for herself. Not being in a position where he wished to argue for too long, Hymie fished £5 from his wallet and hands it over. Several years later, after five children and a long marriage, Hymie returns from work with the bad news that at the end of the week he is being made redundant. He cries, "What are we going to do now?" "Well," says Becky, taking Hymie to the window and drawing back the net curtains, "see that supermarket across the street? That belongs to us, as does the petrol station on the corner and almost the multi-storey car park beyond that. So our income is secure." "How on earth is that possible?" asks Hymie, "and why almost the car park?" "Well," says Becky, "this situation in our lives was always going to happen so all of those fivers that you have given me over the years I have carefully invested. I have bought the supermarket and the petrol station and I have nearly all of the asking price of the car park. Don't you think I am clever?" "Clever?" yells Hymie, "you are not clever, you are stupid!" "How can I be stupid?" replies a bemused Rachel, "I have carefully invested this money for times of insecurity and you call me stupid? How so?" "Stupid," replies Hymie, "because if I had known you were carefully investing the money that I gave you, I would have bought you all of my business."

Hymie's work mates return from lunch with tales of a counter assistant at the local pharmacy offering to assist in finding the customers the correct size of condom – small, medium or large. Eager to discover if this is true, Hymie walks into the pharmacy and asks for a packet of condoms. "What size would that be?" asks the attractive assistant. Feigning total lack of knowledge, Hymie declares that he is not sure, so the assistant takes Hymie to the rear of the store. Afterwards the assistant announces that he is medium and asks how many packets would he like? "None today, thank you," replies Hymie. "I only came in for the fitting."

Hymie recently had cause to visit the police station in Hampstead near where he lives. Looking around he asks, "Who are all of these pictures of?" The constable says, "These are all the people we need to catch." Hymie is a bit confused and asks, "Why didn't you catch them when you were taking their pictures?"

Hymie is not feeling well and goes to the doctors. The doctor examines him and says, "Hymie, I have some good news and some bad news." Hymie says, "I'll have the good news first." The doctor tells him that he has only one day to live. "That's the good news?" cries Hymie. "What's the bad news?" The doctor says, "I should have told you yesterday."

Hymie is walking past a jewellery store when he spots a big gold crucifix in the window. He goes in and asks the assistant, "How much is the crucifix?" The assistant says, "That is 24-carat solid gold and the price is £9,000." Hymie thinks for a minute and then asks, "How much is it without the acrobat?"

Hymie dies and goes to heaven where he sees the long-deceased Rabbi of his synagogue, just as he was in life, old, wrinkled and with a long grey beard. On his lap is the most gorgeous blonde, kissing him. Hymie says, "Rabbi, how is this possible? Is it the reward for a devout and ascetic life?" The Rabbi replies, "No, this is her punishment."

Hymie is crossing a road when he is run over by a hit-and-run driver. A young Catholic priest, seeing him lying there, rushes across to administer the last rites. "Do you believe in God the Father, God the Son and God the Holy Spirit?" he asks. Hymie opens one eye, "You ask me riddles at a time like this?"

A man wearing a bowler hat and pin-striped suit is sitting in a railway carriage reading *The Times*, when he suddenly feels somebody watching him. He lowers his paper and sees Hymie sitting opposite, staring at him. "Oy, oy!" says Hymie, "I think you are a good Jewish boy!" The man glares at him and replies, "Sir, I am not Jewish." This happens again and Hymie says, "Yes! I think you are a Jewish boy." "I am not Jewish," says the man. "Please leave me alone to read my newspaper!" Again he feels the eyes watching him so he lowers the paper, looks around the carriage, sees that nobody is listening and whispers, "All right! I am Jewish but I don't like people to know it." "Funny," says Hymie, "you don't look Jewish!"

Hymie goes to the doctor, "Doctor, I can't stop singing 'Delilah', what's the matter with me?" "You've got Tom Jones Syndrome," says the doctor. Hymie asks, "Is that common, doctor?" The doctor replies, "It's not unusual."

Hymie is discussing with his friends how their religions distribute their charity donations. Bill, a member of the Church of England, says that donations are collected on a silver tray and go towards restoring the church steeple. Pat, a member of the Catholic Community, says that the collections at Holy Communion are distributed to the poor. They ask Hymie how charity donations are collected in his community. "It's like this," comes the reply, "we collect everything in a large box and then throw it up into the air. What the Good Lord wants, he keeps!"

At the synagogue the service is in full swing, when suddenly the Rabbi throws himself to the floor crying, "Lord, before you I am nothing." The Cantor then throws himself to the floor crying, "Lord, before you I am also nothing." Hymie, seeing all this, throws himself to the floor, "Lord, before you I am nothing." The Rabbi turns to the Cantor and says, "Look who thinks he's nothing!"

Hymie goes to see the doctor and asks if he can have some Viagra. "How old are you?" asks the doctor. "Eighty-six," replies Hymie. The doctor tells him that with his health problems and age it is out of the question. Hymie says to the doctor, "Look, I am eighty-six and I would like to see if I can still have some fun. I will take full responsibility if anything goes wrong." The doctor thinks and then says to Hymie, "OK, I will let you have some Viagra but only on the following condition. You must not take it every day. Do you understand? Take it one day, then skip a day and then so on for a month, then come and see me." A month goes by and the doctor is waiting to hear from Hymie, so he calls his home and Hymie's wife answers. "Can I please speak to your husband?" asks the doctor. The wife replies, "I am sorry to say that my husband is dead." The doctor says, "I told him not to take Viagra." The wife replies, "It wasn't the Viagra that killed him, it was the skipping!"

Hymie is on his way to work when he meets his old pal, Monty. "How's things, Monty?" Hymie asks. "Bad," Monty replies, "Ruthie has decided not to marry the doctor, Abie tells me he is gay and Golda is thinking of becoming Buddhist, and," he adds, "business is at an all-time low." "Oh oh," says Hymie. "Mind you, it's not necessarily all bad," says Monty, "this morning at breakfast I buttered my toast, it slipped off the plate, but when I went to pick it up it had landed butter side up! Maybe this is a sign?" "Sure is," says Hymie, "it's a sign you buttered the wrong side."

Hymie goes to a top restaurant and orders the very best from the menu and some bread. He is served with everything plus two slices of bread cut from an exquisite loaf made in the kitchen. Asked at the end about his meal, he replies to the waiter, "Superb, but not enough bread, I only had two slices." A week later, Hymie returns to the restaurant and again orders the very best. This time the waiter cuts four slices of bread from the freshly baked loaf. At the end of the meal, Hymie again remonstrates that there was not enough bread. Next time he is given eight slices cut from the loaf but again tells the waiter that the meal was spoilt by lack of bread. Exasperated, the waiter, on Hymie's next visit, cuts the whole loaf in two and places them on Hymie's table. "Aha!" exclaims Hymie, "I see we are back to two slices."

Hymie visits Moscow for seven days after the fall of Communism in 1991 to see his now free Russian cousin, also called Hymie. Like all Jews, the Russian Hymie had a difficult time in the Soviet Union. Each day of the trip the two Hymies go to the best café in Moscow for breakfast. Each day the Russian Hymie orders a coffee, some cake and a copy of *Pravda*, the Communist Party's daily paper. Each day he is told that he can be served coffee and cake but not *Pravda* as the Communist Party and its newspaper have been abolished by Boris Yeltsin. On the last day, our UK Hymie asks his cousin why he persists in asking for *Pravda*. The Russian Hymie replies, "Because I love being told every day that it and the Party have been abolished!"

Becky, now widowed, goes for her regular weekend in Bournemouth. Among the regular faces she spots a handsome stranger and decides to speak to him. "I haven't seen you here before," she says. "I've been away," he replies. "On business?" asks Becky. "No, actually I was in prison," he replies. "Really, what for?" Becky asks. "I killed my wife." "Oh, so you're on your own?" Becky says.

After the shipwreck, Hymie is clinging to his small piece of wreckage when Abe joins him. "Can't you float alone?" says Hymie. "This is no time to talk business," says Abe.

Hymie and his friend, Abe, are walking through the woods in Georgia when Abe gets bitten on the bum by a deadly snake. As he falls to the ground, he yells at Hymie, "Dial 911! The Snake Bite Centre!" Hymie gets through to a doctor on his mobile who tells him to suck out the poison or else his friend will die. Hymie walks back to his friend who is lying on the ground, who gasps, "What did they say? What did they say?" Hymie looks at his friend sadly and says, "You're gonna die!"

It's Hymie's first day at school. His teacher, Miss Murphy, asks the class, "Who is the greatest man who ever lived, Moses or St Patrick? A shilling for whoever gives the right answer." Hymie says, "St Patrick, Miss." "Well done, Hymie, here's your shilling." After school, Jacob asks him why he said St Patrick. "Vell, you know it's Moses, I know it's Moses, but business is business."

Hymie is locking up his jewellers shop at the close of business. A mugger coshes him over the head and steals the day's takings. As Hymie falls to the ground, bleeding, Moishe, the tailor, rushes over, takes his coat off, puts it under Hymie's head and asks, "Are you comfortable?" Hymie replies, "Comfortable! I've got two shops!"

Hymie's multimillionaire father is taken to hospital after having a heart attack and placed, unconscious, in intensive care. Hymie rushes to the hospital, sits by his father's bedside, distraught. His father regains consciousness. Hymie holds his father's hand and says, "Father, have you any last wishes?" "Yes, son. Take your foot off my fucking oxygen pipe."

Abe tells Hymie that he is going on holiday next week. Hymie says, "Would you bring me back 200 cigarettes?" "Of course," says Abe. On his return Abe gives him the cigarettes. "How much do I owe you for them?" asks Hymie. "£62.50," responds Abe. "Where did you go for your holidays?" asks Hymie. "Scarborough," says Abe.

Hymie and Moishe meet in the street. "Hymie, I'm sorry to hear about that fire in your warehouse," says Moishe. "Ssh!" hisses Hymie, looking furtively over his shoulder, "it's not until next week!" Six months later, they meet again. "Well, Hymie, how's your new warehouse going?" "Oy vey, not so good, Moishe, we were flooded out last week." "So," whispers Moishe, "how do you start a flood?"

Hymie and Becky are in a pub. Hymie says, "I love you." Becky asks him, "Is that you or the beer talking?" Hymie replies, "Neither – it's just me talking to my beer."

With all this new technology regarding fertility, Hymie's 65-year-old wife was recently able to give birth. When she was discharged from hospital and went home, I went to visit her. "May I see the new baby?" I asked. "No, not yet," she said, "I'll make coffee and we can chat for a while first." Thirty minutes passed and I asked, "May I see the new baby now?" "No, not yet," she said. After another few minutes had elapsed, I asked again, "May I see the baby now?" "No, not yet," replied Hymie's wife. Growing very impatient, I asked, "Well, when can I see the baby?" "When he cries," she told me. "When he cries?" I demanded. "Why do I have to wait until he cries?" "Because I have forgotten where I put him!"

Hymie calls on his customer, Malcolm, but when he gets to the shop he finds it has been flooded. A frantic Malcolm is up to his knees in water and sodden cloth trying to rescue rolls of fabric. "Hymie! Help!

What should I do?" "Throw in what you can't sell!" replies Hymie.

Hymie, a 70-year-old wealthy widower, shows up at the Country Club with a breathtakingly beautiful and very sexy 25-year-old blonde, who knocks everyone's socks off with her youthful sex appeal and charm. She hangs on Bob's arm and listens intently to his every word. His buddies at the club are all envious. They corner him and ask, "Hymie, how'd you get the trophy girlfriend?" Hymie replies, "Girlfriend? She's my wife!" They're knocked over but continue to ask, "So, how'd you persuade her to marry you?" Hymie says, "I lied about my age." His friends are fascinated. "What do you mean? Did you tell her you were only fifty?" Hymie smiles and says, "No, I told her I was ninety."

Hymie and Becky take their grandson Daniel to the beach. A wave washes him out to sea. "Oh Lord, save our Daniel," they cry. The next wave deposits him back on the beach. "But he was wearing a hat!" shouts Hymie.

Hymie and Becky are staying at a Jewish hotel in Bournemouth. In the bar, Hymie falls into conversation with a man who is clearly not Jewish. So Hymie asks him why he is staying there. The man says because he actually likes kosher and also because he finds Jewish women very attractive. "In fact," he tells Hymie, "I've had every woman in this hotel bar one." This upsets Hymie, who rushes up to his bedroom where Becky is getting ready for bed. He tells her what the man has just told him, about every woman but one. Becky replies, "Oh, that must be that stuck-up Mrs Sticklegruber."

Cohen can't stand his wife a minute longer. He has to get rid of her. But then murder is illegal, so what to do? He unburdens himself to Hymie. "Cohen, it's no great problem. Vy don't you buy her a car. She can't drive so, who knows, maybe she has an accident and gets killed." So he buys her a little Ford. They meet a week later. "Vell, how did it go?" asks Hymie. "A vaste of money, she drives it perfectly," replies Cohen. "Den take my advice and buy her a Daimler. They're hard to handle so who knows, maybe God vil do a miracle and she vil have a smash and be killed," says Hymie. So Cohen buys her a Daimler. They meet a week later. "Vell, how did it go?" asks Hymie. "A vaste of money. She drives it perfectly," replied Cohen. "Den take my last advice. Buy her a Jaguar," says Hymie. "A Jaguar?" replied Cohen. "Yes," says Hymie, "a Jaguar." So he buys her a Jaguar. They meet a week later. "Vell, how did it go?" asks Hymie. "Vunderful, vunderful! Vun bite and she was finished," said Cohen.

Hymie goes to the doctor in New York. Following a full examination, the doctor tells him, "I got some really bad news, I have to give it straight to you. You only have six months to live." Hymie is shocked and when he recovers his composure he asks the doctor, “Is there any way I can extend the six months?” The doctor looks at him with a resigned expression and says, “Yes, there is one way, go to Florida and marry a Jewish widow. The six months will feel like six years!”

The only cow in Hymie’s small town in Poland stops giving milk. The people do some research and find that they can buy a cow from Moscow for 2,000 rubles or one from Minsk for 1,000 rubles. Being frugal, they buy the cow from Minsk. The cow is wonderful. It produces lots of milk all the time and the people are amazed and very happy. They decide to acquire a bull to mate with the cow and produce more cows like it. Then they will never have to worry about the milk supply again. They buy a bull and put it in the pasture with their beloved cow. However, whenever the bull comes close to the cow, the cow moves away. No matter what approach the bull tries, the cow moves away from the bull and he can not succeed in his quest. The people are very upset and decide to ask their wise Rabbi what to do. They tell the Rabbi what is happening. “Whenever the bull approaches our cow, she moves away. If he approaches from the back, she moves forward. When he approaches her from the front, she backs off. An approach from the side and she just walks away to the other side." The Rabbi thinks about this for a minute and asks, "Did you buy this cow from Minsk?" The people are dumbfounded since they had never mentioned where they had gotten the cow. "You are truly a wise Rabbi," they say. "How did you know we got the cow from Minsk?" The Rabbi answers sadly, "My wife is from Minsk."

Hymie goes to see the Rabbi. "Rabbi, something terrible is happening and I have to talk to you about it." The Rabbi asks, "What's wrong?" Hymie replies, "My wife is poisoning me." The Rabbi, very surprised by this, asks, "How can that be?" Hymie then pleads, "I'm telling you. I'm certain she's poisoning me, what should I do?" The Rabbi then offers, "Tell you what. Let me talk to her. I'll see what I can find out and I'll let you know." A week later the Rabbi calls Hymie and says, "I spoke to her on the phone for three hours. You want my advice?" "Yes," Hymie says. The Rabbi replies, "Take the poison."

Hymie is pushing his shopping trolley around Sainsbury's in Stanmore when he collides with another man's trolley. He says to the other man, "I'm sorry about that. I'm looking for my wife, Becky, and I wasn't paying attention to where I was going." The second man says, "That's OK. It's a coincidence. I'm looking for my wife, too. I can't find her and I'm getting a little desperate." Hymie says, "Well, maybe we can help each other. What does your wife look like?" The man says, "Well, she is twenty-seven years old, tall, with blonde hair, blue eyes, big breasts and is wearing a short skirt and a tight t-shirt. What does your wife look like?" Hymie says, "Doesn't matter. Let's look for yours."

Hymie and his three brothers become very successful. They want to send a 95th-birthday gift to their mother, who lives in Florida. Milton says, "I had a big house built for Mama." Marvin says, "And I had a large cinema built in the house." Maurice says, "I had my Mercedes dealer deliver an SL600 to Mama's door." Hymie says, "You know how Mama loved reading the Bible but now she can't see well enough to do that? I came across a Rabbi who had a parrot that could recite the entire Bible. You name a chapter and verse and the parrot would recite it. I had to give £30,000 to the synagogue but it was worth it." Their mother gets the gifts and sends out thank-you notes. "Milton, the house you built is so huge I only live in one room. But I have to clean the whole house. Thanks anyway." "Maurice, I am too old to travel and all my groceries are delivered. So I'll never use the Mercedes, but thank you for the gesture." "Marvin, you gave me an expensive theatre with Dolby sound and it can hold fifty people. But all of my friends are dead, I've lost my hearing and I'm nearly blind. I'll never use it. Thank you for the gesture just the same." "Dearest Hymie, you were the only son to give a little thought to your gift. The chicken was delicious. Thank you so much."

Hymie is found sitting on the kerbside, head in hands, crying. A passing police officer in his patrol car happens to spot him, stops, winds down his window and asks Hymie, "What's wrong?" "I'm eighty-two years old," says Hymie. "I've been married for three weeks to a 28-year-old woman who insists on making love three times a night." The policeman says, "So what's the problem?" Hymie says, "I can't remember where I live!"

Hymie is sitting on a train reading his paper when the young man opposite asks what the time is. Hymie does not reply so the chap asks again, and again, and again, until he gets so cross that he tears the paper from Hymie's grasp and shouts his request at him. "Look at it my way," says Hymie, "I'll tell you the time and we start to chat. Then we become friends so I invite you home. You meet my daughter and things progress till you want to marry her. Who wants a son-in-law who can't afford a watch!"

Hymie walks into a police station at 10am and says to the duty sergeant, "I would like to speak to the burglar you arrested at 2.30am." The officer says, "This is most irregular. What do you want to speak to him about?" Hymie says, "I want to know how he can get into our house at that time of the morning without waking my wife."

A policeman says to his colleague, "Hymie was shot at close range by his wife." He colleague replies, "If so, there must have been powder marks on Hymie's body." "Yes," says the other cop, "that's why his wife shot him!"

Hymie's friend says to him, "Hymie, I heard you and your wife had a terrible fight the other night. What happened?" Hymie replies, "No problem. She finished up crawling on her hands and knees." Hymie's friend says, "Well done. What did she say?" Hymie replies, "She said, 'Come out from under that bed you snivelling little coward!'"

Hymie is pacing round the bedroom in his very nice house in Manchester. At three in the morning, Becky says, "What's the matter? Why can't you sleep?" He says, "I am worried to death. I owe Morry Cohen across the road £50,000 and I can't pay him." She gets up, opens the window and shouts, "Morry Cohen! Morry Cohen!" Morry opens his bedroom window and says, "What's up?" She says, "My Hymie owes you £50,000 and he can't pay you," then she slams the window down. She says to Hymie, "Now come back to bed and let him worry about it."

Becky and Hymie are celebrating their golden wedding. Hymie asks Becky, "Would you like a new Mercedes?" She replies, "No." He then asks, "Would you like a new holiday home in Florida?" She replies, "No." He then asks, "Would you like to go on a six-month world cruise?" Again she replies, "No." Frustrated, Hymie then asks, "Well what DO you want?" Becky says, "I want a divorce." "My God," Hymie says, "I wasn't thinking of spending that much."

Hymie was sitting next to a fully robed Arab Sheikh on the plane and was pleased that the Arab soon fell asleep. Hymie was a nervous flyer and suddenly felt sick. He was unable to reach the sick-bag in time and threw up all over the Arab. Hymie panicked but thought up an idea. He woke up the Arab, smiled and said to him, "Do you feel better now?"

Hymie says to Benny, "Do you know how to make a Jewish omelette?" "No," says Benny, "how?" Hymie says, "First you borrow six eggs..."

A female CNN journalist hears about Hymie, who has been going to the Wailing Wall in Jerusalem to pray twice a day, every day, for many, many years. To check it out, she goes to the Wall and there he is, walking slowly up to the holy site. She watches him pray and after about forty-five minutes, when he turns to leave, using a cane and moving very slowly, she approaches him for an interview. "Pardon me, sir, I'm Rebecca Smith from CNN. What's your name?" she asks. "Hymie Cohen," he replies. "Sir, how long have you been coming to the Wailing Wall to pray?" she asks. "For about sixty years," he replies. "Sixty years! That's amazing! What do you pray for?" she continues. "I pray for peace between the Christians, Jews and the Muslims. I pray for all the wars and all the hatred to stop. I pray for all our children to grow up safely as responsible adults and to love their fellow man," he says. "And how do you feel, Sir, after doing this for sixty years?" she asks. "It's like talking to a brick wall," replies Hymie.

For years Hymie has been the most generous benefactor of his local synagogue. One evening he decides to dine alone in the town's new French restaurant. Since the menu is in French, he simply chooses the house speciality and, after some time, the kitchen door flies open and a team of waiters march out, led by the head waiter, proudly bearing a whole roasted pig's head with an apple in its mouth. At this point, the Rabbi, who spots Hymie through the window, comes in, is momentarily stunned at the spectacle, but quickly recovers. "Hymie," he says, "look at the way they do their apples."

Seeing the warning light blink on the dashboard, Hymie searches for a refuelling point. He finds a petrol station which doesn't allow self-service but instead has the pumps operated by an attendant. He drives on the forecourt and parks by the pump, while winding the window down. The attendant, who resents having to work on any day, but especially on Sundays, growls, "Juice?" Hymie replies, "As a matter of fact we are, but does that mean we get no fuel?"

Hymie wants to plant his annual tomato garden but it is very difficult work, as the ground is hard. His only son, Vincent, who used to help him, is in prison. The old man writes a letter to his son and describes his predicament: "Dear Vincent, I am feeling pretty sad because it looks like I won't be able to plant my tomato garden this year. I'm just getting too old to be digging up a garden plot. I know if you were here my troubles would be over. I know you would be happy to dig the plot for me, like in the old days. Love Papa." A few days later, he receives a letter from his son. "Dear Papa, don't dig up the garden. That's where the bodies are buried. Love Vinnie." At 4am the next morning, the local police arrive and dig up the entire area without finding any bodies. They apologise to the old man and leave. That same day, the old man receives another letter from his son. "Dear Papa, go ahead and plant the tomatoes now. That's the best I could do in the circumstances! Love you, Vinnie."

Hymie specials for you

If a married Jewish man is walking alone in a park and expresses an opinion without anybody hearing him, is he still wrong?

My father says, "Marry a girl who has the same belief as the family." I say, "Dad, why would I marry a girl who thinks I'm a schmuck?"

Jewish marriage advice: "Don't marry a beautiful person. They may leave you. Of course, an ugly person may leave you, too. But who cares?"

A Jewish woman goes to see her Rabbi and asks, "Yankele and Yosele are both in love with me, who will be the lucky one?" The wise old Rabbi answers, "Yankele will marry you. Yosele will be the lucky one."

The Italian says, "I'm tired and thirsty. I must have wine." The Frenchman says, "I'm tired and thirsty. I must have cognac." The Russian says, "I'm tired and thirsty. I must have vodka." The German says, "I'm tired and thirsty. I must have beer." The Mexican says, "I'm tired and thirsty. I must have tequila." The Jew says, "I'm tired and thirsty. I must have diabetes."

Jewish proverb: "A Jewish-Polish wife will forgive and forget but she'll never forget that she forgave."

Travelling on the night sleeper, Hymie is already in his pyjamas in his cabin when the guard, accompanied by a very beautiful young woman, knocks on the door. "Excuse me, Sir, but there's been a mistake with the bookings and I wonder if you'd mind sharing with this lady?" Hymie gallantly agrees, offers her the top bunk and goes out into the corridor so that she can prepare for bed. When he returns she is already in her bunk, so with a cheery 'goodnight' he gets into his and switches out the light. Some time later he hears her ask, "Are you still awake?" "Yes," he replies. "I'm feeling a bit cold," she says. "Would you like me to get you a blanket?" asks Hymie. "Well," she replies, "I was rather wondering if you'd like to pretend that I was your wife?" "Oh, I see," says Hymie, "get your own blanket then!"

Hymie meets a girl in a bar and after some drinks and conversation he asks, "Aren't you Morry the tailor's daughter?" "Yes," she says. The evening progresses very nicely and eventually they spend the night together. The next day, Hymie calls Morry and says, "Hi, Morry, I've just spent the night with your daughter and congratulations!" Morry says, "You call me to tell me you've slept with my daughter and then congratulations? Why?" Hymie says, "It's the first time you've made something that fits me!"

Hymie speaks with his cousin Isaac, who he hasn't seen for some time. "Hymie, how's the rag trade these days?" "You should ask," says Hymie, "one by one, all the businesses in the street have closed and been bought up by a property developer to build a big new shopping mall." "You sold for a good price?" asks Isaac. "My business has been in the family for over 100 years. I didn't sell even though the developer took over the flats above," says Hymie. "What happened then, Hymie?" asks Isaac. "They built their shopping mall to the left, to the right and over the top of me," replies Hymie. "If trade was difficult before how are you managing to survive with this competition?" asks an incredulous Isaac. "I sell all the same stock and make more profit than ever, but I did change the name of the shop." "What's it called now?" asks Issac. "Entrance," says Hymie.

Hymie returns from India and his close friend asks him, "Did you see the Taj Mahal?" "Yes," he replies, "it's a wonderful building and very beautiful but there's something I don't understand. Why did they name it after my local Indian restaurant?"

Hymie has lived in London all his life but when he graduates from his Jewish school in Golders Green, he decides to go to America and resume his studies over there. Somehow, he manages to get a scholarship to the University of Montana. Although his parents are not happy with his decisions, they know best not to argue with him and so give him their full blessing to go. Six months after Hymie waves goodbye to his parents at the airport, his parents have still heard nothing from him and they are obviously getting quite worried for his safety, especially after they are told by the University that Hymie only attended his course for a few weeks before quitting. Then, one morning, they get a letter from him. Here is what it said: "Dear Mum and Dad, please accept my apologies for not contacting you sooner. I had so much going on over here that I just couldn't find the time. Nevertheless, here is what has happened to me since I left London. On my first day at Montana University, I met the girl who I'm soon going to marry. She's a very special person. That's why I left school for her. Her name is Shining Light. She's not only a Native American, but she's also a real Princess. Her father is the tribe's Chief and I am now a member of the tribe. I also have to tell you something else. I have abandoned the name you both gave me. I am now known to everyone in the tribe as Stalking Bear. I feel so strong about this that I won't talk to or correspond with anyone who calls me by my old name Hymie. I do hope that you will come to accept all of the above." A few days later he gets a reply from his mother. This is what she wrote: "Dear Stalking Bear, your father and I are pleased to learn that you have found a woman to love and cherish. We are also pleased to learn that you are happy to live on the reservation. Although we are obviously sad that she is not Jewish, we nevertheless realise that we can't always have everything. We have also been giving some thought to how we could celebrate your forthcoming marriage to the girl you love so dearly. So we have decided to follow your path. We also have taken Native American names. From now on, I am SITTING SHIVAH and your father is GOING MESHUGGA."

Hymie's favourite joke

An Englishman, a Scotsman, an Irishman, a Welshman, a Latvian, a Turk, a German, an Indian, a New Englander, an Argentinian, a Dane, several Americans (including a southerner and a Californian), an Australian, a Slovakian, an Egyptian, a Japanese, a Moroccan, a Frenchman, a New Zealander, a Spaniard, a Russian, a Guatemalan, a Colombian, a Pakistani, a Malaysian, a Croatian, an Uzbek, a Cypriot, a Pole, a Lithuanian, a Chinese, a Sri Lankan, a Lebanese, a Cayman Islander, a Ugandan, a Vietnamese, a Korean, a Uruguayan, a Czech, an Icelander, a Mexican, a Finn, a Honduran, a Panamanian, an Andorran, an Israeli, a Venezuelan, a Fijian, a Peruvian, an Estonian, a Brazilian, a Portuguese, a Liechtensteiner, a Mongolian, a Hungarian, a Canadian, a Moldovan, a Haitian, a Norfolk Islander, a Macedonian, a Bolivian, a Cook Islander, a Tajikistani, a Samoan, an Armenian, an Aruban, an Albanian, a Greenlander, a Micronesian, a Virgin Islander, a Georgian, a Bahaman, a Belarusian, a Cuban, a Tongan, a Cambodian, a Qatari, an Azerbaijani, a Romanian, a Chilean, a Kyrgyzstani, a Jamaican, a Filipino, a Ukrainian, a Dutchman, a Taiwanese, an Ecuadorian, a Costa Rican, a Swede, a Bulgarian, a Serb, a Swiss, a Greek, a Belgian, a Singaporean, an Italian, a Norwegian and forty-seven Africans walk into a fine restaurant. "I'm sorry," said the maitre d', "but you can't come in here without a Thai."

Hymie goes into a restaurant and orders a steak. After the meal the waitress comes over and asks Hymie how he found the steak. Hymie says, "Easy, I just moved a couple of chips and there it was!"

Hymie is watching golf when a wayward ball hits him on the head. The concerned golfer goes over to check he is OK. "Are you OK?" asks the golfer. "OK?" says Hymie, "I will sue you for £10,000." The caddy interrupts and says, "We shouted FORE, sir." Hymie looks up and says, "OK, OK, I take four."

Hymie says, "Becky, did you know... In the 1880s old Lord Rothschild (the creator of the family seat at Waddesdon) was having a drink in his London club when up came an aged, notoriously reactionary Duke. 'Hello, Rothschild. I'm just back from Japan. Wonderful country. Can you imagine, they have no pigs and no Jews?' 'How interesting, my lord,' says Rothschild, 'next year why don't we go there together. Then they'll have one of each.'"

Hymie is walking down the street with a roll of cloth under his arm. His friend stops him and admires the quality of the cloth. He asks, "What are you going to do with that?" Hymie says, "I'm going to visit Nathan the tailor. He is going to make me a beautiful suit from this cloth." The friend says, "But Hymie, you're a tailor." Hymie replies, "Yes, but I'm too expensive."

Hymie's mother, Mildred, and her lady friend are out driving in a large car. Both can barely see over the dashboard. As they are cruising along, they come to a major crossroad. The stop light is red, but they just go on through. The woman in the passenger seat thinks to herself, "I must be losing it. I could have sworn we just went through a red light." After a few more minutes, they come to another major junction and the light is red again. Again, they go right through. The woman in the passenger seat is almost sure that the light was red but is really concerned that her mind is going. She is getting nervous. At the next junction, sure enough, the light is red and they go on through. So, she turns to the other woman and says, "Mildred, did you know that we just ran through three red lights in a row? You could have killed us both!" Mildred turns to her and says, "Oh! Am I driving?"

A recently widowed Becky bursts into the rec room at the retirement home. She holds her clenched fist in the air and announces, "Anyone who can guess what's in my hand can have sex with me tonight!" An elderly gentleman in the rear shouts out, "An elephant?" Becky thinks a minute and says, "Close enough."

Hymie's mother and a lady have been friends for many decades. Over the years, they have shared all kinds of activities and adventures. Lately, their activities have been limited to meeting a few times a week to play cards. One day, they are playing cards when one looks at the other and says, "Now, don't get mad at me. I know we've been friends for a long time but I just can't think of your name. I've thought and thought, but I can't remember it. Please tell me what your name is." Her friend glares at her. For at least three minutes she just stares and glares at her. Finally she says, "How soon do you need to know?"

Hymie is lying on a beach surrounded by hundreds of other people on loungers. He picks up a mobile phone. A voice says, "Darling, I've been your mistress for twenty years, I've always loved you.

You're the most marvellous man ever. I've just seen a Mercedes that I really need to have. It's £30,000. Please, honey, may I have it?" Hymie says, "Of course you can, my dear." The girl continues, "And precious one, there's a mink coat for sale reduced in price. It's only £25,000 and I really would love to have that. I've wanted a mink coat all my life. Can I buy it?" Hymie says, "You have the mink coat. I think it's a wonderful idea." The girl continues, "And finally, darling, you always said you'd find me somewhere to live. Well, there's a house in Hampstead which is divine. It's £7 million. It's the house that I dream of. Could I buy that?" Hymie says, "You want a house, darling, you buy the house, it's fine with me." The girl says, "You're so wonderful. You're so marvellous. I love you so much. Kiss, kiss, kiss," and she rings off. Hymie holds up the mobile and shouts in a loud voice, "Whose mobile is this?"

Hymie has just gone through a bitter divorce from Becky. He's having a cup of tea with his friend, Abe. Abe asks, "How are you getting on after your trouble?" Hymie says, "I'll manage." Abe asks, "Do you think you'll get married again?" Hymie replies, "Why should I get married again? I'll just find a woman I don't like and give her a house."

Hymie advertises for a wine taster. A local drunk goes in and applies for the job. To try and get rid of him they give him a blind tasting of a dozen wines. His knowledge is perfect in every case. They then decide to give him a glass of urine. He tastes it and says, "25-year-old white. Country of origin, South Australia, blonde, five months pregnant. If I do not get the job, I will name the father."

Becky decides to give herself a big treat for her significant seventieth birthday by staying overnight in an expensive hotel. When she checks out the next morning, the desk clerk hands her a bill for £350. She explodes and demands to know why the charge is so high. "It's a nice hotel but the rooms certainly aren't worth £350 for just an overnight stay! I didn't even have breakfast." The clerk tells her that £350 is the 'standard rate' so she insists on speaking to the manager. The manager appears and, forewarned by the desk clerk, announces, "This hotel has an Olympic-sized pool and a huge conference centre which are available for use." "But I didn't use them," Becky says. "Well, they are here and you could have," explains the manager. He goes on to explain that she could also have seen one of the in-hotel shows for which the hotel is famous. "We have the best entertainers from the world of performing here," the manager says. "But I didn't go to any of those shows," she says. "Well, we have them and you could have," the manager replies. No matter what amenity the manager mentions, Becky replies, "But I didn't use it!" and the manager counters with his standard response. After several minutes' discussion with the manager unmoved, Becky decides to pay, writes a cheque and gives it to him. The manager is surprised when he looks at the cheque. "But madam, this cheque is for only £50." "That's correct. I charged you £300 for sleeping with me," Becky replies. "But I didn't!" exclaims the very surprised manager. "Well, too bad, I was here and you could have."

Hymie and Becky are on a cruise and it is really stormy. They are standing at the back of the ship watching the moon when a huge wave comes up and washes Becky overboard. They search for days but cannot find her so the captain sends Hymie back to shore with the promise that he will notify him as soon as they find something. Three weeks go by and finally Hymie receives an email from the ship. It reads, "Sir, we are sorry to inform you that your wife Becky has been found dead at the bottom of the ocean. We hauled her up to the deck and attached to her butt was an oyster and in it was a pearl worth £50,000. Please advise?" Hymie emails back, "Send me the pearl and re-bait the trap."

Becky and Hymie are going through problems and are committed to a psychiatric institution. After three months there, Hymie falls into the swimming pool. Becky jumps in with great danger to her own life, swims to the bottom of the pool, somehow or other gets Hymie up and on to dry land. The head of the institution sees Becky and says, "It's quite clear that with the action you took you are no longer in need of psychiatric help and therefore the good news is that you can go home. The bad news is that Hymie committed suicide this morning. He hanged himself from a beam in his room." Becky says, "Hymie didn't hang himself. I strung him up there to dry out. Can I go home now, please?"

Hymie goes for a job as a lion tamer. The ring master says, "All you have to do is get into the cage with that big ferocious lion." Hymie says, "Just a minute, what if the big ferocious lion takes a pace forward?" "Simple, just take a pace back," says the ring master. "What if the ferocious lion takes another pace forward?" asks Hymie. "Simple, just take another pace back," replies the ring master. "Just a minute," said Hymie, "what if I am at the back of the cage and the ferocious lion takes a pace forward?" "Simple, just bend forward and throw some manure into the lion's face," replies the ring master. "What if there is no manure?" asks Hymie. "Don't worry, there will be," said the ring master.

Hymie, on his deathbed, says to Becky, "I want to be remembered for a long time." He reaches under the bed, pulls out £30,000 and says with his last breath, "Get a big stone." The next day she tells her friend Rachel, "Hymie gave me £30,000 for a big stone." Showing her hand she asked, "You like it?"

Becky is sitting on a park bench, minding her own business and thinking about nothing much. She is waiting for her husband Hymie to come back from the deli with gefilte fish balls. A strange man walks over to her and stops. "Hello," the man says, "would you like my company?" "I don't know," says Becky, "what do you manufacture?"

Hymie is telling his neighbour, "I just bought a new hearing aid. It cost me $4,000 but it's state of the art. It's perfect." "Really," answers the neighbour, "what kind is it?" "Twelve thirty…"

Hymie and Becky are having dinner at another couple's house and, after eating, the wives leave the table and go into the kitchen. The two gentlemen are talking and one says, "Last night we went out to a new restaurant and it was really great. I would recommend it very highly." The other man says, "What was the name of the restaurant?" The first man thinks and thinks and finally says, "What is the name of that flower you give to someone you love? You know, the one that's red and has thorns." "Do you mean a rose?" "Yes, that's the one," replies the man. He turns towards the kitchen and yells, "Rose, what's the name of that restaurant we went to last night?"

Hymie is driving and is stopped by a traffic policeman. "In a bit of a hurry are we, Sir?" "Well," says Hymie, "I'm late for a circumcision at the synagogue." The officer warms to the opportunity of indulging in some sarcastic banter and cause further delay to poor Hymie. "A circumcision is it? I've always wondered what becomes of the discarded foreskins," queries the policeman. Hymie thinks for a moment and replies, "The Rabbi hangs it on a hook in his office." "What's that for?" asks the puzzled officer. "Every time the Rabbi goes into his office he tugs at the foreskin and stretches it until after several weeks it's about six foot long," says Hymie. "What happens to it then?" "Then," says Hymie, "it joins the police force."

Hymie's family asks the shotchen to find him a good Jewish girl to marry. The shotchen says she knows just the girl – gorgeous, clever, good family etc. Dinner is arranged for the families and the parties to meet. The girl is brought in and is hideous. Hymie grabs the shotchen by the arm, propels her over to the corner of the room and says quietly but firmly, "What are you doing? You said she was gorgeous. She's hideous." The shotchen replies in a perfectly audible voice, "There's no need to visper – she's deaf too."

Hymie's the senior partner of a New York law firm. He's looking for a cab one day outside his office with a young associate when a beautiful young blonde girl walks by. The young lawyer turns to him

and says, "I'd really love to screw that girl." "Out of what?" says Hymie.

Four friends, who haven't seen each other in thirty years, reunite at a party. After several drinks, one of the men has to use the rest room. Those who remain talk about their kids. The first guy says, "My son is my pride and joy. He started working at a successful company at the bottom of the barrel. He studied Economics and Business Administration and soon began to climb the corporate ladder and now he's the president of the company. He became so rich that he gave his best friend a top of the line Mercedes for his birthday." The second guy says, "Darn, that's terrific! My son is also my pride and joy. He started working for a big airline, then went to flight school to become a pilot. Eventually he became a partner in the company, where he owns the majority of its assets. He's so rich that he gave his best friend a brand new jet for his birthday." The third man says, "Well, that's terrific! My son studied in the best universities and became an engineer. Then he started his own construction company and is now a multimillionaire. He also gave away something very nice and expensive to his best friend for his birthday: A 30,000-square-foot mansion." The three friends congratulate each other just as the fourth returns from the rest room and asks, "What are all the congratulations for?" One of the three said: "We were talking about the pride we feel for the successes of our sons. What about your son?" The fourth man replies, "My son is gay and makes a living dancing as a stripper at a night-club." The three friends say, "What a shame. What a

disappointment." The fourth man replies, "No, I'm not ashamed. He's my son and I love him. And he hasn't done too bad either. His birthday was two weeks ago, and he received a beautiful 30,000-square-foot mansion, a brand new jet and a top-of-the-line Mercedes from his three boyfriends."

Young Hymie sits in class as the teacher addresses him, "Hymie, what is 2 per cent of £100?" Hymie doesn't answer. The teacher repeats the question, "Hymie, what is 2 per cent of £100?" Hymie stares straight ahead and keeps schtum. The teacher loses her patience, "Hymie Jacobs! I'm talking to you! What is 2 per cent of 100?" Hymie looks her straight in the eye, "For 2 per cent I'm not interested."

Hymie, a Hasidic Jew, is in Leeds on business. It's now one hour to shabbos and he's all dressed up in his shabbos clothes ready to go to a local shul. He takes the elevator to the ground floor and walks towards the exit. As he reaches the reception area he sees a stunning British Airways hostess with blonde hair and a face and figure you could die for. As soon as she sees Hymie, she stops in her tracks and walks quickly over to him. "Hello," she says to him. "Hello to you, too," he replies. "I have a confession to make," she says. "What is it?" he asks. "I have a sexual fantasy," she says. "Nu, so go on," he says. "I've always wanted to be with a Hasidic man. I want to run my hands up and down his white silk socks, run my hands over his tzitzit and my fingers through his beard, play with his peyess, eat kugel with him, poke my finger in his pippik, remove his gatkes, play with his schlong and then shtup. So, I want you to join me now. I have a room upstairs. What do you say?" Hymie looks at her thoughtfully and asks, "And what's in it for me?"

Hymie and Becky are sitting in their garden in Swiss Cottage. "Becky," says Hymie, "it's your birthday soon, what would you like?" "Well," says Becky, "how about a nice fur coat?" "Fur coat?" says Hymie, "you already have four fur coats." "Well then," says Becky, "how about you get me a car?" "A car?" says Hymie, "you already have a nice little Renault, what do you want another car for?" "You could buy me a diamond ring," says Becky. "Ring, schming," says Hymie, "look at your hands, you don't have enough fingers for the rings you've got." "OK," says

Becky, "just give me £1,000." "Don't be silly," says Hymie, "where do I get £1,000 wholesale?"

As Hymie leaves a meeting at the synagogue he gives himself a pat down. He is looking for his keys. They are not in his pockets. A quick search of the meeting room reveals nothing. Suddenly he realises he must have left them in the car. Frantically he heads for the parking lot. His wife Becky has scolded him many times for leaving the keys in the ignition. His theory is the ignition is the best place not to lose them. Becky's theory is that the car will be stolen. As Hymie bursts through the doors of the shul, he comes to a terrifying conclusion. Becky's theory was right. The parking lot is empty. Hymie immediately calls the police. He gives them the location and confesses that he had left the keys in the car and that it had been stolen. Then Hymie made the most difficult call of all. "Lovey," he stammers, "I left my keys in the car and it has been stolen." There is a period of silence. Hymie thinks the call has been dropped but then he hears Becky's voice. "Doosie," she barks, "I dropped you off!" Embarrassed, Hymie says, "Well, come and get me." Becky retorts, "I will as soon as I convince this policeman I've not stolen your car!"

Hymie and Abe are walking through Central Park when a guy jumps out with a gun and says, "Hand over all your cash or I'll blow your brains out." Hymie says to Abe, "Here's that $100 I owe you, Abe."

Tom, Dick and Hymie attend the funeral of their friend Bob. As the coffin is lowered, Tom throws in £5, "That's the £5 I never had the chance to pay back, old chum." Likewise Dick throws in £10, "That's the £10 you lent me, old pal." Hymie, who owed Bob £50, throws in a cheque for £100, "That's double what you lent me, Bob, I'm a fool to myself."

A Catholic, a Protestant, a Muslim and Hymie are in a discussion during a dinner. Catholic: "I have a large fortune. I am going to buy Citibank!" Protestant: "I am very wealthy and will buy General Motors!" Muslim: "I am a fabulously rich prince. I intend to purchase Microsoft!" They then all wait for Hymie to speak. Hymie stirs his coffee, places the spoon neatly on the table, takes a sip of his coffee, looks at them and casually says, "I'm not selling!"

Hymie is on his deathbed. His son is by his side and asks if Hymie has a last wish. Hymie says he would like a last taste of Momma's apple strudel. His son goes to ask, returns and says, "Momma says the strudel is for after the funeral."

Hymie sells Abe a gross of tinned sardines for 19 shillings. Abe sells them to Moses for 20 shillings. Moses sells them to Samuel for 21 shillings. Samuel sells them to Joseph for 22 shillings. Joseph sells them to Jacob for 23 shillings. When Jacob gets home, Rachel, his wife, asks him what he's been doing all day. He tells her he got a good deal by buying a gross of tinned sardines from Joseph for 23 shillings. Rachel says, "Give me a tin and I'll make us sardine sandwiches." But when she opens the tin, the stench nearly knocks them both out. The sardines are completely rotten. So Jacob complains to Joseph, and Joseph complains to Samuel, and Samuel complains to Moses, and Moses complains to Abe, and Abe complains to Hymie. "Vell," says Hymie, "whadya expect? Those sardines were for buying and selling, not for eating."

Hymie specials

I just got back from a pleasure trip. I took my mother-in-law to the airport.

Someone stole all my credit cards but I won't be reporting it. The thief spends less than my wife did.

We always hold hands. If I let go, she shops.

My wife and I went back to the hotel where we spent our wedding night; only this time I stayed in the bathroom and cried.

My wife and I went to a hotel where we got a water-bed. My wife called it the Dead Sea.

She was at the beauty shop for two hours. That was only for the estimate. She got a mudpack and looked great for two days. Then the mud fell off.

The doctor gave a man six months to live. The man couldn't pay his bill so the doctor gave him another six months.

Doctor: "You'll live to be sixty!" Patient: "I am sixty!" Doctor: "See! What did I tell you?"

A drunk was in front of a judge. The judge says, "You've been brought here for drinking." The drunk says, "OK, let's get started."

Why do Jewish divorces cost so much? They're worth it.

The Harvard School of Medicine did a study of why Jewish women like Chinese food so much. The study revealed that this is due to the fact that Won Ton spelled backward is Not Now.

There is a big controversy on the Jewish view of when life begins. In Jewish tradition, the foetus is not considered viable until it graduates from medical school.

Why don't Jewish mothers drink? Alcohol interferes with their suffering.

Why do Jewish mothers make great parole officers? They never let anyone finish a sentence!

How many Jewish mothers does it take to change a light bulb? (Sigh) Don't bother. I'll sit in the dark. I don't want to be a nuisance to anybody.

Short summary of every Jewish holiday: They tried to kill us. We won. Let's eat.

Did you hear about the bum who walked up to a Jewish mother on the street and said, "Lady, I haven't eaten in three days"? "Force yourself," she replied.

What's the difference between a Rottweiler and a Jewish mother? Eventually, the Rottweiler lets go.

Why are Jewish men circumcised? Because Jewish women don't like anything that isn't 20 per cent off.

Hymie died and his family gather for the reading of his will. "To my wonderful wife, Becky, who shared my life for fifty years, the true love of my life, I leave $5 million. To my son, Sheldon, who helped me run the business and who gave us such 'Nachas', I leave $5 million. To my beautiful daughter, Sophie, who looked after us so well, who entertained all her friends by our pool, I leave $5 million. To my brother-in-law, Manny, who smoked my finest cigars, who drank my best Scotch and who always said that he would never be mentioned in my will, hi there, Manny!"

Hymie is lying in bed, dying. His family are around him. Hymie whispers, "Is all the family here?" "Yes," they all respond. "Then who is looking after the shop?" shouts Hymie.

A jumbo jet has a new crew with a Jewish captain and a Chinese co-pilot. Once the plane is airborne and the computers have taken control, the captain leans back in his seat and says, "I don't like the Chinese." "Why not?" says the co-pilot. "Because they bombed Pearl Harbor," says the captain. "Don't be ridiculous, that was the Japanese," says the co-pilot. "Oh, Chinese, Japanese, they are all the bloody same," says the captain. Silence for two minutes. "I don't like the Jews," says the co-pilot. "Why not?" says the captain. "They sank the *Titanic*," says the co-pilot. "Don't be ridiculous, it was an iceberg," says the captain. "Oh, Goldberg, Rosenberg, iceberg, they are all the bloody same."

Hymie decides to have a three-day break in New York. He checks into the most expensive hotel in Manhattan. He says to the concierge, "Can you arrange an escort for tonight? She must be a nice Jewish girl and the most expensive one in New York." The concierge says, "Yes, but she charges $4,000 per night." "OK," Hymie says. She comes to Hymie's room and takes him to a wonderful restaurant, nightclub and then back to Hymie's room for coffee and a bit of fun. Hymie says what a super time he's had, gives her $4,000 plus a $1,000 tip and asks if she could come back the following night. The next night the same thing: restaurant, nightclub and then back to the hotel for coffee and fun. He pays her $4,000 plus $1,000 tip. Hymie says, "Can you come tomorrow night?" "Of course," she says. The third night, same thing. When Hymie is paying her $4,000 and $1,000 tip she says, "Where are you from in the UK?" He says, "London. Stamford Hill." She says, "I have a sister who lives in Stamford Hill." Hymie says, "I know, she gave me $15,000 to give you."

Hymie has come across hard times and goes to the Wailing Wall to ask God for help. "My wife is ill and I need money for medicine, please let me win the lottery this week." The following week he's there again. "My son's school fees are due and I've no money to pay them, please, please let me win the lottery this week." The next week he's there again. "I've lost my job and now I'm going to lose my home, please, please, please let me win the lottery this week." Suddenly God appears before him. "Hymie, meet me halfway – buy a ticket!"

A Mexican maid asks for a pay increase. Becky is very upset about this and decides to talk to her about the raise. She asks, "Now, Maria, why do you want a pay increase?" Maria says, "Well, Senora, there are tree reasons why I wanna increaze. The first is that I iron better than you." Becky asks, "Who said you iron better than me?" "Jor huzban he say so," says Maria. "Oh yeah?" says Becky. "The second reason eez that I am a better cook that you," says Maria. "Nonsense," says Becky, "who said you are a better cook than me?" "Jor huzban did," replies Maria. Becky, getting increasingly agitated, says, "Oh, he did, did he!?" "The third reason is that I am better at sex than you in bed," says Maria. Becky, really boiling now and through gritted teeth, says, "And did my husband say that as well?" "No, Senora," says Maria, "the gardener did." "How much do you want?" asks Becky.

Hymie's daughter gives birth to his first grandchild. He rushes to his club and proudly announces the birth of his first grandson weighing at birth a whopping 18lb, and buys drinks all round. He returns a month later and on being asked about his grandson and his weight now he says, "He is fine and now weighs 10lb." His pal says, "Golly, has he been ill to lose all that weight?" Hymie replies, "No. He has been circumcised."

Times are hard and Hymie and his wife Becky are having a furious argument about money, or the lack of it. "We've simply got to economise somehow," says Hymie, "if only you could learn to make meals properly, we could sack the cook." "In that case," says Becky, "if only you could learn to make love properly, we could sack the gardener."

Hymie is unexpectedly home for the day and the phone rings, which he answers, "Sorry, my friend, I think you want the coastguard." "Who was it?" asks Becky. "Some guy wanting to know if the coast is clear," replies Hymie.

Hymie and Becky are having a quiet romantic dinner in a fine restaurant chosen by Michael Winner. They are gazing lovingly at each other and holding hands. Their waitress, taking another order at a table a few steps away, suddenly notices Hymie is slowly sliding down his chair and under the table, but the woman is acting unconcerned. The waitress watches as the man slides all the way down his chair and out of sight under the table. Still, the woman appears calm and unruffled, apparently unaware her dining companion has disappeared. The waitress goes over to the table and says to the woman, "Pardon me, ma'am, but I think your husband just slid under the table." The woman calmly looks up at her and says, "No, he didn't. He just walked in the door."

Hymie and Becky are at an entertainment night at the Old People's Home. Claude the hypnotist declares, "I'm here to put you into a trance. I intend to hypnotise each and every member of the audience." The excitement is palpable as Claude withdraws a beautiful antique watch from his coat pocket. "I want you each to keep your eye on this antique watch. It's a very special watch. It's been in my family for six generations." He begins to swing the watch gently back and forth while quietly chanting, "Watch the watch, watch the watch, watch the watch..." The crowd become mesmerised as the watch sways back and forth, back and forth, light gleaming off its polished surface. Hundreds of pairs of eyes follow the swaying watch until, suddenly, it slips from the hypnotist's fingers and falls to the floor, breaking into a hundred pieces. "Shit!" says the hypnotist. It took three days to clean up the Old People's Home. Claude was never invited back.

Two ducks called Hymie and Becky decide to go away for a dirty weekend at a big country hotel. They arrive at the hotel and check in as Mr and Mrs Duck. They are shown to their room where they unpack their suitcases. Becky says to Hymie, "Do you fancy making mad passionate love to me?" "Of course I do," says Hymie. So they jump into bed together and Hymie gets very passionate with Becky, kissing her all over. He is just getting ready to perform the finale when Becky utters the immortal words, "Hymie, have you got any protection? You are not coming near without some." Hymie gets all flustered and asks Becky where he might obtain this. Becky suggests that he rings room service and ask them to send one up to their room. So Hymie leaps out of bed and dials room service. "Hello, room service? This is Mr Duck in room 477, er, I wonder if you could send up a pot of tea for two and, er, could you also send up a condom please?" "Certainly sir," came the response. After about five minutes there is a tap on the door, "Room service," and the door opens. A waiter enters with a tray and the requested tea and condom. As the waiter places the tray down on the sideboard, he looks at Hymie and says, "Would you like me to place this on your bill, sir?" Hymie, shocked, replies, "What kind of pervert do you think I am?"

Hymie says to Abe, "Close the curtains next time you make love to Rachel, the whole street was watching last night and they're all laughing about it." Abe replies, "The joke's on them. I wasn't even home last night."

Becky has bought a magic mirror at a local market. Hymie is keen to try it out. Wishing to improve his love life, Hymie stands naked in front of the mirror and utters the magic words, "Mirror, mirror, on the wall, make my penis touch the floor." It worked. His legs fell off.

Hymie is getting some stick from his wife. "We're so cramped living here. What this house needs is a cellar." Hymie replies, "What this house needs is a buyer."

It is parents evening at little Oscar's King David's primary school. Hymie says, "His reading is OK but we're worried about his numbers." Rabbi replies, "His Numbers? You should see his Deuteronomy."

Hymie is being interviewed for a job. The HR man asks, "Are you able to cope with change?" Hymie replies, "Sure, but I prefer notes."

Hymie is walking around the Serpentine in Kensington Gardens when he trips and falls in. Hymie, who cannot swim, is extremely lucky to be pulled out by the balls. Hymie, who is recuperating from the ordeal, would like sincerely to thank Mr and Mrs Ball.

Hymie dies. Some months later at the stone-setting everyone is surprised to see the name 'Becky' on his tombstone. The Rabbi explains that Hymie's accountant had recommended him to put everything in his wife's name.

Little Hymie and his Czechoslovakian friend go to the zoo and sit on the wall of the lion's den. Hymie's friend falls over and is swallowed by a lion. The keeper arrives and asks which one swallowed him. Hymie points to the one with the big mane. On slicing it open, no friend. One by one the lionesses are opened and from the fourth out jumps the boy. Motto: never believe a Jew when he says, "There's a Czech in the male."

Hymie is talking to an old friend. "The only things Becky and I ever argue about are money and sex." "Money AND sex?" asks his friend. "Yes," says Hymie, "I reckon she charges me too much."

After working for many years at Hymie's restaurant, Moishe, a much loved waiter, passes away. He is missed so much by his customers that a group of them go and visit a spiritualist to see if they can contact Moishe in the afterlife. The psychic tells them to go back to the restaurant and bang on the table as they did when Moishe used to serve them, and he will appear. The group knock on the table harder and harder, but nothing happens. They begin to call his name, more and more loudly, and suddenly, there is Moishe coming towards them with the menu. "What happened, Moishe?" asks one of the group, "why didn't you come when we first began knocking?" "This wasn't my table," replies Moishe.

As Hymie leaves the synagogue, his friend sees him and says, "Hymie, why do you look so sad?" "Oh," says Hymie with a sigh, "on the way here I found a pay packet on the pavement." "Hymie, that is a stroke of luck!" his friend exclaims, "you should be happy with such fortune." "Yes," wails Hymie, "but did you see how much tax was deducted!"

The Commander of the Cossacks brings his troops to a halt in the middle of a poor village and stares in amazement at the door of a large barn. It is covered in bullet holes, each exactly in the centre of every target on the barn door. He barks out orders to fetch the village headman and within minutes the man stands in front of him. "Headman, bring me the marksman who did this," says the Commander. "Sir, I dare not, he is the village idiot. You don't want to see him," says the village headman. "Bring him to me now or you will pay with your life. What is his name?" asks the Commander. "His name, Sir, is Hymie the Idiot, I will fetch him," says the headman. Hymie the Idiot is brought before the Commander who, gesturing towards the barn door, demands, "Did you do this?" "Yes, Sir, I did," replies Hymie. "Then you will come with me and teach the soldiers of the Czar how to shoot," says the Commander. "But Sir, you don't understand, Sir, first I fire the shot and then I paint the target," says Hymie.

Having spent a fortune on a name change and an artificial foreskin, Hymie plays his first round of golf. He sinks his final putt and throws his arms in the air shouting, "Oy vey!" quickly adding, "Whatever that means."

Hymie is sitting on a park bench with Becky. Becky says to Hymie, "What do you think of Fay?" Hymie says, "Why do you always have to talk about this one and that one? Have you not got anything topical or interesting to say?" Becky says, "What do you think of Red China?" Hymie replies, "Lovely with a blue tablecloth."

Hymie and Becky's son is expelled from the local Jewish school for uncooperative behaviour. He is then sent to one further away. Again, he is expelled after a couple of months. A third one across the city is found. He lasts only a couple of weeks. Hymie, in despair, goes to the headmaster of the local Catholic school, who agrees to do his best. Transformation. Shoes clean, hair neat, on time, homework carefully done, excellent marks. After six weeks, Hymie and Becky can stand the suspense no longer. "Maurice," they ask, "why the transformation?"

Maurice looks at them sharply. "Mum, Dad, don't you know? They've one of us, nailed up on the dining room wall."

A teacher notices that Hymie Jr is at the back of the class squirming around, scratching his crotch and not paying attention. She goes to find out what is going on. He is quite embarrassed and whispers that he has just recently been circumcised and he is quite itchy. The teacher tells him to go down to the principal's office. He is told to telephone his mother and ask her what he should do about it. He does and returns to his class. Suddenly, there is a commotion at the back of the room. She goes back to investigate only to find him sitting at his desk with his 'private part' hanging out. "I thought I told you to call your mum!" she says. "I did," he says, "and she told me that if I could stick it out until lunchtime, she'd come and pick me up from school."

Hymie is at hospital awaiting the arrival of his new son. The doctor comes out to tell him the birth has been a success apart from one thing – he doesn't have any eyelids. Hymie is distraught until the doctor says there is one type of operation they can do if he wants them to. Hymie asks, "What is it?" The doctor replies, "If we were to circumcise him, we could use the skin as eyelids." "Great," says Hymie. The doctor replies, "There is only one problem: he will be cock-eyed."

All is not well between Hymie and Becky and they agree on a trial separation. In need of a solid break, Becky books herself on an African safari. The third day into the jungle, she is swept off her elephant's back by an enormous gorilla. He carries her to his

lair, where he has his evil way with her, several times a day, for months, until one day she is spotted aimlessly wandering around by another safari party and promptly rescued. Although she has been back in London for a while, Becky is still distraught. Her best friend, Miriam, takes her out to lunch. "Becky, darling, you are safe now, it's all going to be fine." "Oh Miriam, that's easy for you to say (sob) but he doesn't phone, he doesn't write…"

Hymie, suffering from depression, visits the psychiatrist. "You should look at the positives," says the shrink. "You've got more money than Bernie Madoff." "I suppose I have," says Hymie, "that's good." "You're held in higher esteem by your family and friends than Ryan Giggs," the shrink continues. "That's true, that's true," he's forced to concede. "And you're better looking and better dressed than Michael Winner." "Oh come on," says Hymie, "everyone is better looking and better dressed than Michael Winner."

Three elderly men, Hymie, Abe and Moishe, are discussing their night-time problems. Hymie says, "I always wake up at 6am and have to take a pee. My bladder is causing me agony but all I can produce is a tiny thin dribble that comes and goes for ages and gives me no relief." Abe chimes in, "Well, at 6am every day I wake up and feel I have to take a shit. I strain and strain but all I can ever produce is one tiny dried-up turd. The pain is terrible and passing the turd is agonising. They turn to Moishe, "What about you?" "Well, at 6am every day I pee like a racehorse and produce a great fountain with no effort. At the same time, quite painlessly and with no straining, I have an enormous shit," says Moishe. "So what's the problem then?" they ask. "I don't wake up 'til 9am."

Hymie, on his first visit to Orlando, Florida, finds the red light district and enters a large brothel. The madam asks him to be seated and sends over a young lady to entertain him. They sit and talk, frolic a little, giggle a bit, drink a bit, and she sits on his lap. Hymie whispers in her ear and she gasps and runs away. Seeing this, the madam sends over a more experienced lady to entertain the gentleman. They sit and talk, frolic a little, giggle a bit, drink a bit, and she sits on his lap. Hymie whispers in her ear and she too screams "No!" and walks quickly away. The madam is surprised that this ordinary-looking man has asked for something so outrageous that her two girls will have nothing to do with him. She decides that only her most experienced lady, Lola, will do. Lola has never said no, and it's not likely anything would surprise her. So the madam sends her over to Hymie. They sit and talk, frolic a little, giggle a bit, drink a bit and she sits on his lap. He whispers in her ear and she screams, "NO WAY, BUDDY!" and smacks him as hard as she can and leaves. The madam is by now absolutely intrigued, having seen nothing like this in all her years of operating a brothel. She hasn't done the bedroom work herself for a long time but she's sure she has said yes to everything a man could possibly ask for. She just has to find out what this man wants that has made her girls so angry. Besides, she sees a chance to teach her employees a lesson. So she goes over to Hymie and says that she's the best in the house and is available. She sits and talks with him. They frolic, giggle, drink and then she sits in his lap. Hymie leans forwards and whispers in her ear, "Can I pay in Euros?"

Hymie's tax inspection

At the end of the tax year, the Tax Office sends an inspector to audit the books of a synagogue. While he is checking the books he turns to the Rabbi and says, "I notice you buy a lot of candles. What do you do with the candle drippings?" "Good question," notes the Rabbi. "We save them up and send them back to the candle makers, and every now and then they send us a free box of candles." "Oh," replies the auditor, somewhat disappointed. But on he goes, in his obnoxious way, "What about all these bread-wafer purchases? What do you do with the crumbs?" "Ah yes," replies the Rabbi, realising that the inspector is trying to trap him with an unanswerable question. "We collect them and send them back to the manufacturers and every now and then they send us a free box of bread wafers." "I see," replies the inspector, thinking hard about how he can fluster the know-it-all Rabbi. "Well, Rabbi," he goes on, "what do you do with all the leftover foreskins from the circumcisions you perform?" "Here too, we do not waste," answers the Rabbi. "What we do is save all the foreskins and send them to the Tax Office and about once a year they send us a complete prick."

A circus owner runs an ad for a lion tamer, and two people show up. One is Hymie in his late sixties and the other is a gorgeous blonde in her mid-twenties. The circus owner tells them, "I'm not going to sugar coat it. This is one ferocious lion. He ate my last tamer so you two had better be good or you're history. Here's your equipment – chair, whip and a gun. Who wants to try out first?" The girl says, "I'll go first." She walks past the chair, the whip and the gun and steps right into the lion's cage. The lion starts to snarl and pant and begins to charge her. About halfway there, she throws open her coat to reveal her beautiful naked body. The lion stops dead in his tracks, sheepishly crawls up to her and starts licking her feet and ankles. He continues to lick and kiss her entire body for several minutes and then rests his head at her feet. The circus owner's jaw is on the floor. He says, "I've never seen a display like that in my life." He then turns to Hymie and asks, "Can you top that?" "No problem," says Hymie, "just get that lion out of there."

Hymie dies and goes to heaven. God greets him on arrival and says, "Why do you look so sad when you should be happy to be here in heaven?" "Well," responds Hymie, "I have a big regret: my only son turned Christian and I did not know how to deal with it." "Funnily enough," says God, "I had the same problem as you." "And how did you solve it?" asks Hymie. "I made a new testament."

A Jewish girl brings her fiancé home to meet her parents. After dinner, her mother tells her father to find out about the young man. The father invites the fiancé to his study for schnapps. "So what are your plans?" the father asks the fiancé. "I am a Torah scholar," he replies. "A Torah scholar," the father says. "Admirable, but what will you do to provide a nice house for my daughter to live in, as she's accustomed to?" "I will study," the young man replies, "and God will provide for us." "And how will you buy her a beautiful engagement ring such as she deserves?" asks the father. "I will concentrate on my studies," the young man replies, "God will provide for us." "And children?" asks the father. "How will you support children?" "Don't worry, sir, God will provide," replies the fiancé. The conversation proceeds like this and each time the father questions, the fiancé insists that God will provide. Later, the mother asks, "How did it go?" The father answers, "He has no job and no plans, but the good news is he thinks I'm God."

Hymie buys a fabulous home in Beverly Hills, California. He brings in a local workman to decorate the place. When the job is finished, Hymie is delighted but realises that he's forgotten to put mezuzahs on the doors. He goes out and buys fifty mezuzahs and asks the decorator to place them on the right-hand side of each door except bathrooms and kitchens. He's really worried that the decorator will chip the paintwork or won't put them on correctly. However, when he comes back a few hours later, he sees that the job has been carried out to his entire satisfaction. He's so pleased, that he gives the decorator a bonus. As the decorator is walking out of the door he says, "Glad you're happy with the job. By the way, I took out all the warranties in the little boxes and left them on the table for you!"

Yeshiva University decides to field a rowing team. Unfortunately, they lose race after race. Even though they practise and practise for hours every day, they never manage to come in any better than dead last. Finally, Hymie tells the team to send

Morris Fishbein, its captain, to spy on Harvard, the perennial championship team. So Morris schleps off to Cambridge and hides in the bushes next to the Charles River, where he carefully watches the Harvard team at its daily practices. After a week, Morris returns to Yeshiva. "Well, I figured out their secret," he announces. "What?! Tell us! Tell us!" his team mates shout. "We should have only one guy yelling. The other eight should row."

More Hymie specials

It is mealtime during an ELAL flight. "Would you like dinner?" the flight attendant asks Hymie, seated in the front. "What are my choices?" asks Hymie. "Yes or no," she replies.

A Rabbi is opening his mail one morning. Taking a single sheet of paper from an envelope he finds written on it only one word: "schmuck". At the next Friday night service, the Rabbi announces, "I have known many people who have written letters and forgot to sign their names, but this week I received a letter from someone who signed his name and forgot to write a letter."

Signs on Synagogue Bulletin Boards:

UNDER SAME MANAGEMENT FOR OVER 5,763 YEARS.

BEAT THE ROSH HASHANAH RUSH, COME TO SHUL THIS SHABBAT.

DON'T GIVE UP. MOSES WAS ONCE A BASKET CASE!

COME EARLY FOR A GOOD SEAT.

What part of "Thou shalt not" don't you understand?

Becky goes to the post office to buy stamps for her Channukah cards. She says to the clerk, "May I have fifty Channukah stamps please?" "What denomination?" says the clerk. Becky says, "Oy vey, my God, has it come to this? OK, give me six orthodox, twelve conservative and thirty-two reform."

Hymie goes to Israel to attend a recital and concert at the Moscovitz Auditorium. He is quite impressed with the architecture and the acoustics. He inquires of the tour guide, "Is this magnificent auditorium named after Chaim Moscovitz, the famous Talmudic scholar?" "No," replies the guide. "It is named after Sam Moscovitz, the writer." "Never heard of him. What did he write?" "A cheque," replies the guide.

Hymie is reading the paper and comes upon a study that says women use more words than men. Excited to prove to Becky, his wife, his long-held contention that women in general, and his wife in particular, talk too much, he shows her the study results, which state: "Men use about 15,000 words per day but women use 30,000." Becky thinks a while then finally she says to Hymie, "That's because we have to repeat everything we say." "What?" says Hymie.

Hymie is taking an oral exam while applying for his citizenship papers. He is asked to spell "cultivate" and he spells it correctly. He is then asked to use the word in a sentence and, with a big smile, responds, "Last vinter on a very cold day, I vas vaiting for a bus but it vas too cultivate, so I took the subvay home."

The three Cohen brothers, Hymie's ancestors, Norman, Hyman and Maximillian, invented and developed the first automobile air-conditioner. On

17 July 1946, the temperature in Detroit was 97 degrees. The three brothers walked into old man Henry Ford's office and sweet-talked his secretary into telling him that the three gentlemen were there with the most exciting innovation in the auto industry since the electric starter. Henry was curious and invited them into his office. They refused and instead asked that he come out to the parking lot to their car. They persuaded him to get into the car, which was about 130 degrees, turned on the air-conditioner and cooled the car immediately. The old man got very excited and invited them back to the office where he offered them $3 million for the patent. The brothers refused, saying they would settle for $2 million but they wanted the recognition by having a label "The Goldberg Air-Conditioner" on the dashboard of each car that it was installed in. Now, old man Ford was more than just a little bit anti-Semitic and there was no way he was going to put the Goldberg's name on two million Ford cars. They haggled back and forth for about two hours and finally agreed on $4 million and that just their first names would be shown. And so, even today, all Ford air-conditioners show on the controls the names "Norm", "Hi" and "Max".

Hymie is at the grocer's. "How much are those?" he asks. "Two for £1," comes the reply. Hymie asks, "How much for one?" "Seventy-five pence," says the grocer. "I'll have the other one then."

Hymie is out for a few drinks with some friends and has had a few too many beers and a fair amount of a rather nice pinot noir. Knowing full well he may have been slightly over the limit, he does something he's never done before. He takes a bus home. He arrives safely and without incident – which is a real surprise. He'd never driven one before.

Becky says to Hymie, "Look, I haven't worn this for twenty-four years and it still fits me." Hymie responds, "It's a bloody scarf!"

Becky goes upstairs one morning to wake Hymie, only to find he has died. She rushes out on the landing, leans over the banisters and calls loudly, "Rosa, Rosa, only two eggs."

HYMIE AWARDS

"OK, Hymie, now we'd like you to give your Awards."

"Vy should I give out Awards?"

"Because we often do that."

"Vell, suppose you always go to the North Pole? I'm not going there and how can I give out Awards, I never go anywhere?"

"I'll help you, Hymie."

"So you mean they're not my Awards, they're your Awards?"

"No, Hymie, they're your Awards, I'll just give you the nudge. Now, what restaurants do you like?"

"Vell, I like Reubens in Baker Street and I like Reubens in Baker Street and I'm very fond of Reubens in Baker Street. They do wonderful mixed soup, lockshen and kneidlach and very good gefilte fish."

"Well, there must be another restaurant you like as well, Hymie?"

"No, there isn't. That's the only place I go other than when I eat at home. Becky's a good cook, you know."

"This could make it difficult for you to give Awards, Hymie."

"Difficult? Makes it impossible. I don't give for nothing about Awards anyway. They're for schlemiels. They're not for nice Yiddisher people such as me."

"Well, Hymie, if I put you on the rack like they did in the Spanish Inquisition and insist that you tell me what restaurants you like other than Reubens, what would you say?"

"They could pull me apart. They could tear me limb from limb. There's nothing else I can say. I hate restaurants. I hate waiters. I hate receptionists. I never go out except to Reubens."

"Oh right, Hymie, instead of choosing restaurants let's choose people you admire in the restaurant business."

"How can I admire someone in the restaurant business when I don't go to restaurants? What's wrong with you? You're a total schlemiel."

"Well, I'm just trying, Hymie. We've got to get something out of this. It says the Hymie Awards so there has to be Hymie Awards."

"All right, guide me. Tell me somebody I might like."

"Well, there's Richard Caring."

"Richard who? I've never heard of the putz."

"He's a very nice young man, beautifully dressed, runs some of the finest restaurants in London."

"What do I care? I never go to them."

"Doesn't matter. He's a great success in the restaurant and hotel business. I think we should give him an honour."

"You give him an honour. What honour can I give him?"

"We'll name him Man of the Year or something."

"You can name him Schmuck of the Year, makes no difference to me."

"Then there's Chris Corbin and Jeremy King."

"What are they? A stage act? Do they sing? Do they dance?"

"No, no, they're also very famous restaurant owners."

"They mean nothing to me."

"Yes, but Hymie, I think we should give them an Award too."

"So we're giving all your friends Awards, is that how it is? And you're giving them Awards and I'm meant to be the one who has agreed to this. I do not agree to it. I've never heard of these people. I don't want to know them. I don't want to see them."

"Well, Hymie, the Awards are given out each year by very famous people. Michael Caine gives out an Award."

"Michael Caine the actor? Now there's a mensch. That's a proper person. He's an actor. He can act. And he's a commoner. He's a cockney. He's almost as common as me."

"Yes, Hymie, that's true. And then they're also given out by Andrew Lloyd Webber."

"Oy, I love Andrew Lloyd Webber. His music is fantastish. What's that song he did from the show? Sunrise and sunset, sunrise and sunset, goes on like this."

"That's from *Fiddler on the Roof*, Hymie."

"Yes, that's right. *Fiddler on the Roof*."

"Lord Lloyd Webber didn't write *Fiddler on the Roof*."

"He didn't? Vy not? What did he write?"

"He wrote *Jesus Christ Superstar*."

"Jesus Christ is not a Superstar in our household. What did he write we might know, this Lloyd Webber?"

"*Cats.*"

"We don't like cats."

"*Joseph and his Technicolor Dreamcoat.*"

"Vhat? The man has a coat? He's writing about the schmutter business? I've never heard of that either."

"And then we've had Joanna Lumley give out these Awards."

"Ah, now there's a beauty, Joanna Lumley. Becky would love to meet Joanna Lumley. She'd like to congratulate her on all she did for the Indians."

"She didn't do anything for the Indians, Hymie. She pioneered to get the Burmese who'd fought for the British during the war accepted into this country."

"Nepalese, Schepalese, Indian Schmindian, what's the difference? Becky would like to meet her."

"And then we've had Sir David Frost give out these Awards."

"Sir David Frost? Who's he? I've never heard of David Frost. Is he in a Christmas play? Does he come on with icicles all over him? Never heard of him. Couldn't care less about him."

"But Hymie, he's a very important person. He interviewed Richard Nixon."

"Well, he interviewed Nixon. That's his business. Nothing to do with me. Nixon means nothing to me. Frost means nothing to me except for when it's cold, then I put on an overcoat and then I go out in the cold and I say it's frosty but I'm wearing my overcoat, doesn't matter."

"And then we've had Roger Moore give out these Awards, Hymie."

"Roger Moore? The James Bond? He lifts an eyebrow. He thinks that acting. Vhat do I care an ex-James Bond? I didn't care when he was James Bond. I like the Scots fellow. What was his name? Conville? Gonville?"

"Connery."

"Ah yes, Connery, I liked him. After him, I didn't care for any of them. Becky liked him too. She didn't want any of the others."

"Hymie, I don't think you're taking this seriously. We have to get some other people. So far we've only got Corbin and King and Richard Caring. It's not enough."

"Vell, you're so clever, you think you're a food critic. You think you know everything. You're an absolute schlemiel but you think you know everything. You think up some people. Let me know when you think them up and I'll discuss it with Becky."

"And I've got some other ideas, Hymie, there's a very senior Italian restaurateur called Arrigo Cipriani and I think we should give him an Award."

"An Italian? I don't do Italy. We went to Tel Aviv once but there were no Italians there. Why should we give this Cipriani fellow an Award?"

"Well, he's got Harry's Bar in Venice, he's got some of the finest restaurants in the world, he's a black belt and he's over eighty years old."

"This is a reason to give him an Award? Sounds a reason to give him a wheelchair."

"No, no, Hymie, he's a very, very significant and lovely person. We'll give him an Award. And I'll tell you someone else. We might include another Italian called Maurizio Saccani who manages the greatest group of hotels in Europe, the Orient Express and Italian Hotels."

"Orient Express? I thought that was a train."

"Yes, they have a train as well, Hymie."

"That train, that's where people keep getting

murdered, isn't it? Murder on the Orient Express. Is it safe to take this train?"

"Hymie, you're being extremely flippant about this. I'm suggesting some very senior people who deserve our fullest respect."

"*Your* respect they may deserve, my respect they haven't got because I don't know who they are. But you know, to keep you happy, Michael, since you're such a pain in the toches, if you like them, I like them. That's until I meet them and don't like them."

"Thank you, Hymie, I knew you'd be reasonable about this."

"Tell me, Michael, will you have a party to give Awards out to these people? If so, Becky and I better start preparing. Becky's got a dress she wore for my son's bar mitzvah, I think she could still get into that. Maybe she will have to let it out a bit. So we want to be prepared."

"I'm not sure if I'm going to give a party or not, Hymie."

"Vy not give a party? They give a party for your Awards, why can't they give a party for my Awards?"

"Well, they're not really your Awards, are they, Hymie? You've really done nothing to create them and you haven't been very helpful in coming forth with people anyway."

"Vell, one good turn deserves another. If you have a party, I want a party. I'm going to make out a list of people you should ask. There's the Chief Rabbi, there's my local Rabbi, there's Moishe Pippick who lives a couple of doors away from me, there's Abe Schwantz, one of my dear friends. Yes, I can get a good list of people I want at the party. Becky's relations would fill the room. You tell me that date so we can all get ready for the party."

"Hymie, I'm not guaranteeing you a party. We may not give out the Awards; we may just leave them announced in the book."

"Who cares about the book? Who cares about the Awards anyway? I guess they might care about the party. The whole thing is a complete waste of time, Michael. But then you like wasting time. That's part of your main activity in life. You could put under hobbies 'wasting time'. I, on the other hand, am a very busy man. I've got two schmutter shops, a wife, a number of children, all this keeps me quite occupied."

"I'll let you know about the party, Hymie. Leave it with me."

"How can I leave decisions regarding a party with you, Michael, you're inept, you don't know what you're doing, when you're writing, how would you know how to run a party? In my house we know how to run a party. You should have seen the party we gave for my son, Abe's bar mitzvah, dis was a party. We had 150 people in the garden, in a tent, all the catering was kosher, the food, you should have seen the food, there was enough food for 600 people and we only had 150 and they ate all the food. Then we had an Israeli folk orchestra and people were dancing, you should have seen them dance. Moishe Pippick's father was so old that he dropped dead dancing. Nobody noticed, they just danced all over him. This was what I call a party."

"But I'm not even sure we're having a party, Hymie."

"Well, if you're anything to do with it, it's probably better that we don't. If you put Becky in charge of the party, you'd see a party. She'd ask all her friends. There's Mrs Cohen from next door, there's Rachel Schwantz from a couple of blocks away, we've got a lot of friends. Some of them are very peculiar but we can't have friends that are all normal. Becky could do the whole party, she could do the catering, she could do the guests. In fact, for an extra couple of quid under the table, she'd stay and do the washing up."

"I think you're going on about this party far too much, Hymie. I don't think you deserve a party, really, I mean your jokes are funny, some of the things you say are funny, most of them by mistake, but I don't think any of it merits a party."

"What, you don't think I'm funny? Of course I'm funny compared to you. I'm hysterically funny. Compared to you, a dead gorilla's funny, compared to you, a decaying frog is hysterical. The trouble with you, Michael, is somebody said you were funny and you believed them. They've said you know how to write and you believed them. This is a problem you have, it's what we call in Yiddish clever dick."

"Clever dick is not Yiddish, Hymie, it's English words, I'm sure there's a Yiddish word for it but I don't happen to recall it at the moment."

"Schwitzer, Michael, that's the word, and that's what you are! Either way, Michael, you are not funny and you are not very intelligent. You don't look any good any more. Quite honestly, there's not much point in having you around at all. If I give a party, it's not necessary for you to be there."

"Well, that's the first good thing you've said, Hymie, so if there is a party at least I don't have to waste time going to it."

"Ha, that's a typical schwitzer remark. My father was King of the Schmutter, now I'm King of the Schmutter, you're King of the Schlemeils."

"Hymie, I think you're being very ungrateful. I gave you a book, your name is on the cover of the book, your opinions are scattered throughout the book."

"They're not my opinions, they're jokes."

"Well, they concern you and they've got your name on them."

"So what if they've got my name on them, they're jokes. I didn't do those things and now you're having a big say at the end about the Awards which we aren't going to give out anyway. That's terrific of you, that's really nice of you, Michael. I have a big say about something that isn't going to happen, that's what I call really generous, that's what I call shmo talk. You're a typical shmo, probably not even Jewish."

"Hymie, I was bar mitzvah'd at the orthodox synagogue in St Petersburg Place."

"Well, no one would know, Michael, nobody would know. In fact bar mitzvahing you was a waste of time for the Jewish race. I don't know why they bothered."

"Because my parents were very proud, Hymie, they wanted to see me confirmed in the Jewish faith."

"Oy, what schmucks your parents were as well. They want to see you confirmed in the Jewish faith! You're no more Jewish than the Pope. Mind you, I've always thought the Pope was Jewish. I've always said to myself that Pope is Jewish, the way he walks about like he's dressed with a little skullcap on his head. If that's not a Jew I don't know what is and they call him a Pope. I wouldn't call him a Pope, I'd call him a Jew."

"Yes, well, Hymie, not everybody would be of that opinion."

"They don't understand, do they? They must have had a Pope that was a Jew, there's probably quite a few of them, although it's not a good job for a Jewish boy. What does he do? He walks about in a long gown. He waves his arms about. He stands on a balcony and everyone starts looking up at him and dovening, praying. This is not a real occupation like owning schmutter shops or selling shoes. That's a job, selling shoes, being a Pope is not a job."

"Hymie, I'm not sure how we got into this, it really doesn't matter whether the Pope's a Jew or not a Jew or whether he's got a nice job or not according to you, because you don't know what you're talking about."

"Now, you want to talk about a job, the Chief Rabbi's got a job. He's trying to keep in touch with and maintain the Jewish community. That's a job, that's a saintly thing to do and what thanks does he get for it? Nothing! I bet the Chief Rabbi gets paid less than my assistant in my schmutter shop in King's Cross. Complete waste of time being a Rabbi when the Chief Rabbi's even more of a waste of time, because you spend years and years struggling to achieve the peak of your profession and, when you get there, you get £1.80 a week – if you're lucky. They have to fill the charity box to pay you and nobody wants to give any money to charity particularly to Chief Rabbis. I'll tell you what's a good job, Michael, being an Ayatollah. An Ayatollah, there's a job! Not necessarily a job for a Jewish boy, but there's a job. They strut about, they come out with pronouncements. They want to bomb Israel, they want to bomb

America, they want to bomb everything. They've just got a lot of hatred in them but they are Ayatollahs. That's what I call a proper job, they're dedicated."

"Hymie, I think you're getting completely into the world of fantasy. Having a conversation with you is like trying to push a jelly up a hill."

"Whoever tried to push a jelly up a hill? You're a schmuck, Winner, nobody pushes jelly up a hill, you push it down the hill. You let it roll down the hill of its own accord, you don't push a jelly up a hill. What schmuck would try and push a jelly up a hill? I suppose you and your gentile friends would try and push a jelly up a hill. What's the purpose of pushing a jelly up a hill? What happens when you get to the top? You say, 'Oy, I've reached the top of the hill and there's a bit of jelly left, let's all sit down and eat jelly on top of the hill'. I've never heard of anything so stupid in my life. Down the hill is different. You roll the jelly down the hill. You end up in a nice green field, you sit in the field and someone brings out some plates and then you eat the jelly and you have a bit of cream with it and maybe you have some fruit with it. That's what I call a little repast at the bottom of the hill. Mind you, if you're not careful, other people pushing the jelly down the hill will push their jelly all over you. You'll be sitting there having your jelly in the field with your little plates and napkins and suddenly you'll be deluged in jelly. You'll be covered in jelly because other schmucks like you are pushing the jelly down the hill. Do you ever eat jelly?"

"I eat jelly all the time, Hymie. I like jelly very much."

"Well, that's because you're a putz. You like jelly as it slithers down the throat. No problem, you don't need teeth, well, you're too old for teeth anyway, Michael, you don't need teeth for jelly, all you need is a spoon and, wollup, it's down. It really is sitting in your stomach doing no good to anybody. It wasn't doing any good before it hit your stomach either so if it's doing no good what's the point of pushing it up a hill or what's the point of rolling it down a hill? I don't know why people have this fetish about jelly. Now a nice piece of gefilte fish I can understand. But nobody would push gefilte fish up a hill and then roll gefilte fish down a hill. There's no point in it and furthermore they'd be swept aside by people pushing jelly. Who wants to mix gefilte fish and jelly? Ridiculous. You're meant to be a food expert, Michael, tell me, does gefilte fish go with jelly?"

"I'd rather not comment on that, Hymie."

"Of course, you'd rather not comment on it because you've got no brain and you know nothing about food and you know nothing about gefilte fish and you know nothing about jelly. You call yourself a food expert and some newspaper prints your nonsense every week like you're important. They print your photograph and if that hasn't frightened the readers off I don't know what will. At least you've got a beautiful shiksha wife – there's a nice-looking woman. They should print her photograph every week and leave yours in the dustbin. I don't mean to be rude, Michael, I'm just ruminating on life. There's no point in your photograph being in the paper and there's no point in you being in the paper. There's not much point in you being anywhere at all, quite honestly. You could go to a nice rest home somewhere and rest. That's what I think you should do at your age, find a nice rest home. It doesn't matter whether it's a Jewish rest home or a Catholic rest home or an Ayatollah rest home, just rest, just sit there, Michael, and look out of the window and rest. The trouble with you is you think it's important to keep your brain working. You don't have a brain, so it's not working but you think it is working."

"Hymie, this conversation is getting very unpleasant."

"Unpleasant, what's unpleasant? I'm only putting a few home truths to you, Michael. There was no point in you being bar mitzvah'd, there's no point in you pretending you're a Jew, there's no point in you writing newspaper articles. You should just be in a home. Becky knows some homes. Her grandmother was in a home for a long time in Stanford Hill, quite a nice home, if you like a lousy view of a rundown street. But I suppose you want a home in the country, you want to look out on a flower garden, you want to look out on trees and peacocks. Well, you can't really be Jewish if you want that sort of thing, the Jews settle down, all they care about is when's lunch, when's dinner, when's breakfast, is the cooking any good, is the food any good? I don't know why I'm planning your life for you, Michael, it's over anyway, there's no point in planning it."

"Thank you, Hymie, that's very sweet of you."

"Yes it is sweet of me because I'm thinking of your future, however brief it is. I'm thinking of you in a home. I'm going to ask Becky to look up some nice Jewish homes because she had a whole lot of brochures when her Aunty Sylvia had to go in a home and I'm sure, knowing Becky, she kept the brochures, even though some of them are so old that the homes have been pulled down and turned into swimming pools."

"Hymie, we were originally discussing whether we should give out your Awards."

"I don't want my Awards given out! I haven't decided on any Awards, I don't like Awards. All I want is an Award from the bank for having a lot of money, that's the only Award that interests me. You know my philosophy of life, Michael?"

"I hate to think, Hymie."

"My philosophy of life is this and it's a true story. Back in Russia, we lived in a village. There was a wise man of the village and he sat thinking for three years. After thinking for three years, he called the villagers around him and he said, 'I've made some very important decisions and I've made a major discovery. Life is a cherry tree.' One of the villagers shouted out from the back row, 'Absolute nonsense, I've never heard such rubbish in my life.' At which point the wise man says, 'OK, life is not a cherry tree.' Would you agree, Michael, that sums up life?"

"Well, it's not bad actually, Hymie, coming from you, that's quite good."

"Thank you, Michael, I knew we'd find some common ground at last. I think we should say goodbye now, to you, to me, to the readers, if we've got a reader. If there's a reader left he's stupid, if there's a reader still reading this rubbish he deserves to be put away, he doesn't even deserve to be in a home, he deserves to be in an asylum, but if there's any readers left we can say goodbye to them. Goodbye, readers."

"Thank you, Hymie, I will join you in that statement."

"What statement? I didn't make a statement."

"Well, it sounded like a statement to me."

"Well, that shows what a schmuck you are."

"As one schmuck to another, Hymie, here are eight of my funniest restaurant reviews. I know you'll love them."

MY FAVOURITE COLUMNS

Hymie, rather than talk about humour, I'm going to give you an example of my wonderful humour, brilliantly written and superbly put together. These are some of my favourite columns that appeared in the *Sunday Times*. I know that you will love them, Hymie, because you are a man of taste, well, you're not a man of taste, but you may well love these reviews anyway. If you don't, quite honestly I don't give a damn.

Cipriani Hotel

The finest group of hotels in Europe are the Orient-Express Italian hotels. There's the Villa San Michele in an old monastery just outside Florence, the Splendido in Portofino overlooking the stunning little bay, the hotel Caruso on a hill top in Ravello and the recently added Villa Sant'Andrea and the Timeo in Sicily. These are run by the elegant Vice President of Orient-Express Italy, Maurizio Saccani. The jewel in the crown of this collection is the Hotel Cipriani in Venice surrounded by luxurious gardens and with an enormous swimming pool. I've vacationed there for over forty years. On my recent visit, while it remains great, things were a bit odd. Geraldine noticed the salad bar by the lagoon seemed lifeless, normally it displayed a home-made mayonnaise and a pink seta rosa sauce: these were missing. I asked the general manager Giampaolo Ottazzi why. His response was "They must have forgotten." "I've been here six days, they can't forget for six days," I reasoned. Thereafter, the sauces sometimes appeared, sometimes did not. I phoned Carlo Lazzieri, the superb food and beverage manager of their sister hotel the Splendido. "We have them out every day," he confirmed. "How many jams do you provide on the breakfast tray?" I asked. "Six," said Carlo. The Cipriani offered three. When I told Mr Ottazzi, he again looked confused. If I pointed out anything, he said, "I'll look into it." He's the general manager. It's his job to know what's going on and why. Giampaolo is very charming and solicitous, even though his black-and-white two-tone shoes are a bit much. Room service at the Orient-Express hotels has always been near perfect. This time, when I ordered breakfast, I was asked to hold. Another Italian staff member came on. “He didn’t understand your order,” he said, referring to the man who’d just taken it. I went through it all again, slowly and carefully. Half an hour later, a lady rang, “The people you spoke to didn’t understand your order,” she said. So I went through it all again. In a two-week stay, of the twelve breakfast orders, at most, two came in correctly. I told Mr Ottazzi and got the usual answer, “I’ll look into it.” In general, the food was very good, nothing better than the amazing cocktails they offer. I had them without alcohol for reasons I won’t go into. The liver veneziana is perfect, the green tagliolini with ham and cheese memorable. Most memorable was when I ordered, at the poolside, roast chicken. They have a special chef for those restaurants, Roberto Gatto (“have microwave, will travel”). He produced the worst main course I’ve ever been served. Dried up, over micro-waved slabs of chicken – totally inedible. How dare a grand hotel come up with a fiasco like that? Most of the staff were excellent, Roberto Senigaglia, who greets people from the boats, is exemplary; management material if ever I saw it.

The concierge who meets me at the airport, Maurizio Caracciola, is also extraordinarily good. The hotel has six restaurants, it's still superb, but at the moment the staff are deciding what and when to perform. The place appears to be run by a headless chicken. Maurizio Saccani should sort this out.

China Tang

I've always found the staff at China Tang in the Dorchester hotel to be surly, unwelcoming and a total pain. So, before my recent visit, I emailed the owner Sir David Tang and asked if he'd give them a good bollocking. Whatever he did had no effect, they were still as dreadful as ever. The restaurant itself is exceedingly handsome, decorative glass pillars, wall paintings of fish and an alcove done as a library, full of Chinese books. Majestic as the room is, in a large restaurant at lunchtime it lacked customers. Other than our table – me, Geraldine and my assistant Dinah – there never seemed to be more than ten other people. This made the experience rather gloomy, added to by the gloom and doom of the staff headed by restaurant manager, Peter Horton. Not a sign of warmth or a decent welcome. Odd really, because Sir David himself is full of charm, smiles and vivacity. None of which he has managed to imbue in his staff. The food was superb to good. The ladies thought it the best Chinese food they'd ever eaten. I was disappointed they didn't have fried seaweed or prawn crackers – two of my favourites. I started with dim sum: fine but not historic. Geraldine had the biggest tiger prawn I've ever seen, Dinah had soft-shell crab. They were ecstatic about them and the rest of their food. I thought my sweet and sour pork was historic, the chicken in black bean whatever, particularly good. The crispy duck wasn't crispy enough, the meat clumsy. I've had better in many other Chinese restaurants including previously at China Tang. The boiled whale was very tasty. Whale is becoming an exceedingly popular dish. Only the other day, Her Majesty the Queen said, "Charley, darling, you are my son and hair (geddit hair not heir, little joke there), nip down to the Thames at Runnymede and catch mumsy a nice whale for lunch." So the son and hair took his little net, the one he used on family holidays in Bridlington, donned his waders and went down to the Thames with six lackeys and – lo and behold – came back with this enormous whale. "Goody, goody," exclaimed her Maj, "put this in the fridge and we'll have it for a few days." "It's too big for the fridge, mumsy," explained Charley. "Buy another fridge," ordered her Maj. "You know," said Charles, "As the whale is a protected species, do you really think you should be eating one?" "Nonsense, Charles," said her Maj, "there are 12,000 whales in the ocean, I know because Philip checked it on the internet, 12,000 is quite enough whales. Any more and they'll take over the world." Meanwhile, back at China Tang, the ladies still cooed over how great the food was. I said to the surly waiter, "Order me a toffee apple, it'll be ready by the time the ladies have finished." It wasn't. I waited and waited. I got every pathetic excuse, "It's on its way." "Where from, Australia?" I asked. "It'll be with you in seconds." It wasn't. "It's only a toffee apple," I said incredulously. "How can anyone spin that out to a twenty-minute wait?" They did.

PS: We didn't really eat whale, that was just a bad-taste joke.

Imperial

I'm no expert on Golders Green but I have a soft spot for it. Why, I can't imagine. Nobody I know ever lived there. If I've driven through more than a dozen times I'd be surprised. I like the comfortable domestic houses. Not flashy like Hampstead, not Dallas-style gross like the monstrosities in nearby Bishop's Avenue or Winnington Road. Thus seduced by my imaginary aura of a halcyon GG, I decided we'd drop in somewhere for Saturday lunch. Boy, did I have a wrong number. Saturday is the Jewish holy day, the shabat. I had no idea there were so many frummers (frummer: a deeply religious Jew) in the area. Shops, restaurants, nearly everything was shut. Even the Carmelli bakery where once I bought a great bagel was shuttered. Geraldine observed, "I was thinking it would be like St John's Wood High Street which is super. This is a mouldy street." This was a view echoed by an old Jewish lady sitting outside Imperial, one of the few places open. "This street used to be the Bond Street of north-west London, but it's changed. Charity shops, lot of tat, it's gone downhill. My childhood has disappeared," she announced sadly. We went into Imperial, regardless. It's a pleasant, wooden-floored café. The brochure said, "We proudly serve Union brand hand-roasted coffee, a powerful yet very velvety mix of Latin, African and Indonesian Arabica beans. Our milk is heated to around 65 degree as we feel this enhances the milk and espresso. This releases the natural sugars in the milk. We do not boil milk, which obliterates the subtle flavours." Bet you didn't know that. I asked the extremely charming Iranian manager, Sean Naghibi, if this could be described as a Jewish restaurant. "The owner is Jewish but it's not kosher," explained Sean, "his wife's Italian. She makes our jam." Outside the window, Archie's Supermarket was closed. Geraldine said, "He's obviously Jewish. His real name is Aaron." The food at Imperial was remarkably good. I started with superb hummus followed by chilli con carne, which Sean told me was made on the premises. It sat on a plate of yellow rice. Very nice, too. Geraldine had the house salad: chicken strips, green bean and soy beans with mint vinaigrette, mayo-free coleslaw, apple and cucumber, toasted cashews with thyme and coriander dressing sprinkled with feta cheese. She reported, "I've rarely had such a tasty salad ever." My dessert was a scone (heavy), homemade allotment jam (historic) and their Union coffee, which was fantastic. Geraldine had hers black amd liked it so much she asked for another. When we came out, a Borough of Barnet parking ticket was affixed to the Bentley. Obviously the parking attendant was not a frummer.

PS: Nearby is a café-bakery called the Old Tree which is run by oriental people. I bought a butter bread roll (cloying) and some almond biscuits (excellent). Overall, a strange experience. Nothing wrong with that.

Dabbous

It's always interesting to me – in truth not interesting at all – when two highly intelligent food writers visit the same restaurant and come away as if they went to two totally different places. Last week, my highly distinguished colleague A. A. Gill reviewed Dabbous in London's Whitfield Street. He gave it the maximum number of stars for both food and atmosphere. I've never seen such rave reviews for a restaurant. On their website, Faise Masie, our most distinguished critic, called it a "game changer". Gilesey Pilesey, who looks so elegant, called it "indescribably good, cooking 9/10". Guy Dimond (never heard of him) in *Time Out* said, "The extraordinary dishes with their sometimes earthy or even metallic flavours are as cutting edge as you'll find." If I want metallic flavour, I'll stay home and eat nuts and bolts. I thought it was like a student restaurant at Cambridge, when there were electricity cuts: dark, the next table six inches away. It's claustrophobic. We were in a corner away from the window, the walls moving in on us. I could be taken away by the men in white coats before I get the food. I said to the charming manager Graham Burton, "If I mention Coca-Cola will I be asked to leave?" We were given a paper bag of warm seeded sourdough bread. Michael said, "It's the best bread ever." We got cashew nuts which they smoke on the premises. Nuts were served in profusion. Every course seemed to contain chopped nuts. If someone came in allergic to nuts they'd drop dead within five seconds. Diners would simply stumble over them to get to their tables. I got six sticks of asparagus and a sauce. No knife and fork, just a fingerbowl. I don't like eating with my fingers. The mayonnaise with the asparagus was good. My salmon was so tiny you could pick up a bit of celery and put it over the top and it'd be completely hidden. I said to Shakira, "I'm not going to eat all my salmon, that'll shock the chef because I'm sure nothing's ever come back to the kitchen before." Geraldine said, "Yours won't, I'm going to eat it." My dessert was a triumph. Gave me faith in the chef-owner Ollie Dabbous. It was iced lovage, like a green sorbet. Lovage is a herbaceous perennial plant, cultivated since the time of Pliny (23–79AD) when it was a general remedy for sore throats and an aphrodisiac. I know it as the title of the 1981 play written for Maggie Smith – *Lettice and Lovage*. Maggie got the Tony award for Best Actress in it. I must ask her if she knew it could also be a sorbet. I was with Maggie at the Cipriani hotel in Venice. She looked around at the assorted guests and said, "Darling, there can't be anyone left in Kyoto."

Quo Vadis

Soho ain't what it used to be. In the 1950s and early 60s, I had an office and a movie cutting room there. It was wonderful. Like a village. There was Jack Carlton with his Prego coffee bar, where I went every morning at 11am and had a bagel with smoked salmon and a cup of tea. Jack later found his wife in flagrante with one of his waiters at another restaurant he owned in Marylebone. He left Old Compton Street. Next to him was Cyril Henry the hairdresser, a very small, fat Jewish man with a gargantuan blonde shiksa (non-Jewish) wife. She went off. Cyril left. Next to Cyril was the Soho Record Centre owned by Alex Strickland. He and his wife Josie stayed together. On the corner of Old

Compton Street and Dean Street, Jack Spot, a well-known Jewish gangster, and Albert ('Italian Al') Dimes, a renowned enforcer, had a fight in broad daylight, slashing at each other with old-fashioned open razors. Very messy. A bit further down Dean Street was a mambo club run by a nice man, Mr France. I went there one day to see him. He lay in a pool of blood on the floor. Probably hadn't paid his protection money. At the bar of Wheeler's in Old Compton Street, I sat at lunchtime with Francis Bacon and Lucian Freud. In those days I had a tiny office in Dean Street next to Don Arden (né Levy), father of Sharon Osborne. He was bringing US acts over. I met 'Great Balls of Fire' Jerry Lee Lewis and his 13-year-old child bride, plus many others. Don Arden famously hired the Everly Brothers for a UK tour. In those days, pop concerts offered ten or so acts each doing about fifteen minutes each. Don's show was on the road when he decided he didn't need the Everly Brothers, who were the costliest act on the bill. He got people to go to the gig and boo and shout "Go back to America" and other nastier things. So the Everly Brothers said, "They don't like us here," and quit. Those were the days. Now Soho is overcrowded, full of pseuds fighting to get into the Groucho Club. The movie companies, who had great window displays all up Wardour Street, have gone. The ladies of the night (and day) have decamped. I try to avoid Soho. I was tempted back three times to vist Quo Vadis in Dean Street. The first when Marco Pierre White took it over, bringing Fernando Pere from the Ivy as restaurant manager. Fernando held tables back for celebrities at every meal service. They never turned up. Marco sold the place. Two very posh brothers, Eddie and Sam Hart, took over. I tried it again because everyone said they'd made it so good. It was OK. I went to a birthday party in their private room and it was the most incompetent debacle ever. As Eddie explained when I was in recently, they were serving food that cost too much to buy and was too expensive for the clientele. So, in January this year, they changed course. It's now cheap and moderately cheerful. Much as I admire Sam and Eddie I still find the premises close to revolting. White walls, hard surfaces, ghastly lighting. Noisy beyond belief. But nice for the Hart brothers as it seems to be doing well. My starter was hare soup. Odd. Not unpleasant. Wouldn't order it again. Then I had rabbit and duck pie. Hearty stuff. Pastry on top like rubber. They should get someone from the Woman's Institute, they're brilliant at pastry. Seeing I'd left most of my pie, Eddie explained, "Pies are designed for rugby players in their twenties." If I meet a 20-year-old rugby player, I'll ask him if he likes rubber pastry. When my dessert arrived the waiter said, "Excuse me, sir, your little lemon posset." He wasn't kidding. It was in a tiny bowl not much bigger than an egg cup. Geraldine was pleased with her liver. I wish Sam and Eddie great good fortune. They're lucky people. They won't see me in Quo Vadis again. In fact, I'll never be in Soho again either.

PJ'S

Brian Stein, who you've never heard of, owns this 'n' that. Sticky Fingers, Café de Paris, the Jewish blind school. He might be distantly related to Hymie, through his aunt's niece once removed. If the niece is like my relatives, she should be totally removed. To be serious (why?) Brian, a charming man, also owns PJ's, a brasserie in the Fulham Road. I was asked there to lunch with Brian, his beautiful Chinese lady friend Platina Tong, Mr and Mrs Bill Wyman (Mrs didn't show) plus the elegant and lovely Geraldine Lynton-Edwards. It's an attractive room, a bar with a clock behind it and a royal crest. Are you royalty, Brian? You kept that quiet. There's reddish wood, slatted floors, mirrors – looks like an old pub. Photos of polo on the wall. Brian plays polo. He's cracking on, but game. I asked the waiter if they could squeeze some oranges for me. "We get it in freshly squeezed," he responded. That's absolute rubbish; it comes in plastic containers, not fresh in any known language. They squeezed some for me. Bill Wyman entered. Thankfully, he'd stopped dying his hair jet black. It's delightfully grey-white with a brown patch at the back. "Is that a moustache?" I asked. Bill replied, "I haven't shaved for a week." PJ's produced Kingsdown Water. I complained. I'd already complained about the orange juice. "Difficult, isn't he?" observed Brian. "You ain't seen nothing yet," I told him. I started with classic Caesar salad. Very good, but took forever to arrive. Bill got a mushroom risotto with glumpy slices of cheese on top. He can't tolerate coffee or cheese. Normally they give you the risotto, then ask if you want cheese on it. There was a delay while it was changed. I ordered a White Park beef sirloin, medium rare, with Béarnaise sauce. Francesco Manzari, the restaurant manager, said, "It's a rare breed from the north of

England." "Where in the north of England?" asked Bill, "is it from near Carlisle?" Francesco had no idea. This was like asking him about atomic fusion. Bill persisted, "Is it over Hadrian's Wall, that side or this side?" "He can find out where it comes from, make a phone call," I advised. Francesco returned and said, "The beef is from Dorset." "I've got news for you," I said, "Dorset is not in the north of England." Brian said, "He's Italian. They always get the north and the south confused." My steak came just before I died from old age. Francesco asked, "How are you enjoying your food so far?" Brian immediately responded, "Very good, thank you." "He's the owner, what do you think he's going to say?" I announced. The steak was first rate, very tasty. I don't know what the taste was but it was unusual and a delight. Bill loved his risotto. I finished with a marvellous apple crumble with rum and raisin ice cream. The food at PJ's is excellent. But the service, oh dear. We came in at 1pm. By 2.30pm I didn't even have my dessert. And the place was far from full. If it's busy, bring a tent, cos it'll be an over-nighter. Sorry for taking the mickey, Brian, but as the saying goes: you shouldn't join if you can't take a joke.

PS: Bill was speaking of the upcoming fiftieth anniversary of the Rolling Stones. He stopped playing with them years ago. They want him back for the anniversary tour. Bill, wisely, said he didn't want to tour, why not have a single concert at Madison Square Garden, New York, sell it to HBO and take the money without having to go round boring hotels? If it happens that way, it'll be the first scoop I ever had. Prefer a scoop of vanilla ice cream though.

Chicago Ribshack

People often ask, "What's the worst meal you ever had?" Takes me a while to choose. Now I can answer in a second. The worst meal I ever had by a long way was at the Chicago Ribshack in Knightsbridge. What a total, unmitigated disaster. As Geraldine was in Paris I took, with her permission of course, my assistant Dinah May. As you go up the stairs to enter, there's a neon sign which reads, "Wait here I've gone to get help". On the right there's a wall of model pigs with a red neon sign saying "EXH'PIG'TION". That should tell you everything. We sat in a red-leather (or fake leather) booth facing a chipped table. Above us were a large plastic lampshade and four bulbs. One bulb wasn't working. The lampshade was dirty with what looked like congealed ketchup. The menu read, "We hope you like our modern take on the iconic Rib Shack." Our waiter, Henrique, wouldn't give his second name. "Work for the secret service do you?" I asked jovially. I was capable of joviality because at that point I hadn't eaten. There was "the chef's classic tender baby back ribs". "It's done so it falls off the bone," explained Henrique, "so it's much easier." Then, "meaty St Louis cut ribs". "That's taken from the front of the pig," said Enrique, "you get more meat but it's much tougher to eat and it sticks to the bone." Finally there was "beef ribs cooked with the Shack's secret recipe to make them fall off the bone". I ordered the beef ribs, but Henrique firmly suggested I had the classic tender back ribs, "They fall off the bone much easier," he explained. I settled for that. When my ribs arrived they did not fall off the bone because there didn't seem to be any meat to fall off. I sawed away with a steak knife. Got an occasional sliver of tough and nasty pork. The ribs were totally useless. Henrique said the meat would fall off. There was nothing falling off. You'd need a circular saw to get any off. A lady appeared, probably the manager. "There's no meat on this and the tiny bit there is doesn't come off," I said. "Would you like a replacement?" asked the manager. "No, I can't order twice," I responded. Prior to this horror I'd been served another fiasco. Potato skins filled with melted cheese and sprinkled with spring onions. "Add grilled bacon or jalepeno peppers for no extra charge." These were vastly unpleasant. Skins were soggy, cheese and whatever not just tasteless but actively nasty. I got the impression they'd hung about in the kitchen far too long. I gave a bit to Dinah. She pulled a face and moved her head from side to side, looking grumpy. "Oh my God. Tastes awful," was her verdict. Henrique saw my plate of uneaten potato skins. "You're not happy with the skins?" he asked. I just raised my hand in an imperious manner. "Why not try the vanilla cheesecake," Dinah suggested, "that sounds as if it could be all right." It was unspeakably awful. Heavy, far too much gelatine in it and it also seemed not very fresh. I had difficulty swallowing. Dinah took some, said, "It's absolutely dreadful, and the potato skins were disgusting." It was all worse. Dinah had smoked salmon which was OK and a filet steak that was overdone. At £33.70 inc. service charge for an 8oz steak it was, to put it mildly, high. Dinah's little cup of blue cheese dressing brought the comment, "If I was blindfolded I couldn't tell what this was, it's just a creamy nothing." The bill for this atrocious so-called meal was 2p short of £80. Outrageous. Not surprising that there seemed to be only twelve diners. I never realised that anywhere, let alone in Knightsbridge, such abominable food was being served.

La Genova

It's always disappointing to be disappointed. I went to La Genova in Mayfair seeking fun and food, full of hope. It started thus: I was meeting Jeffrey Archer to take his photo for this column. He was lunching at La Genova with Norman Lamont. Jeffrey had never been there. He assured me it was John Major's favourite restaurant. Nice man, John. If he recommends a restaurant, run. I went in with Jeffrey and we ordered a fruit cocktail. The most horrific, probably tinned, muck was presented to us. But the place looked lovely. Very old-fashioned, nice tables, nice chairs, nice trolleys of starters and desserts, everything was nice. The staff was particularly nice. They'd all been there for years. The owner, Rinaldo Perrini, aged eighty-two, wandered about in an apron like an Italian version of S. Z. 'Cuddles'

Sakall. Geraldine and I returned later for Saturday lunch. On the way in were framed photos of John Major; I didn't recognise any of the others although one was captioned Isla Blair so I guess it was her. A regular customer said, "That's Tony Bennett's table." He's Italian, I thought. Real name Anthony Benedetto. I looked closely at the two trolleys; one had big shrimps, sea food salad, mushrooms, one had the most gorgeous-looking strawberries. I took one. Best strawberry I'd ever eaten and it was well out of strawberry season. It came from Belgium. We sat in comfortable chairs at a nice table. Everything's nice here. Except the food. I started with the shrimps. Tasted like processed paper. The bread was tired and they had wrapped Anchor butter. I was not put on earth to unwrap butter. "What was I put on earth for?" I asked Geraldine. "One wonders," she replied, later changing to, "You were put on earth for me." My main course liver Veneziano was cloggy, poor texture, tough, no great taste. I ate a bit and gave up. Geraldine had grilled salmon (£30.37 inc. service) which was so dry and overcooked, she couldn't eat it. She took my liver, observing it had too much vinegar in the sauce. Luckily I'd also ordered spaghetti (Agnesi from

Liguria) with tomato sauce. That was fine. The room was so cold even Geraldine, who likes cold, asked them to raise the heating. For dessert, I played safe with the Belgian strawberries, which encircled some very flat raspberries. The chef, Giovanni Turnes, has been there nineteen years. He should get out a bit and see what other Italian restaurants are offering. In case you're thinking, "This is a low-priced local restaurant, why be so tough on it?" the bill for two was £150.75. Only alcohol consumed: a Bellini and one glass of white wine. As we left, Geraldine said, "The reason nobody knows this place is because it's not very good." Some people know it. Apparently a large group had booked downstairs for the night we were there. To each his own.

PS: S. Z. 'Cuddles' Sakall was a lovable Hungarian, famous for playing Carl the head waiter in *Casablanca*. He was known for the phrase "Everything is hunky-dunky." S. Z. specialised in excitable theatrical impresarios, lovable European uncles and befuddled shopkeepers. He supported stars such as Errol Flynn, Gary Cooper, James Cagney and Doris Day. They don't make 'em like that nowadays.

Hymie phones his mother and asks, “How are you?” She says, “Fine.” He says, “I must have the wrong number.”

Also available from The Robson Press

TALES I NEVER TOLD!

MICHAEL WINNER

Michael Winner is a man who has lived with the stars and through extraordinary experiences. He was, for a while, the youngest movie director in the English language and his career has included decades in Hollywood, producing and directing some of the most famous films of the twentieth century, including the *Death Wish* series.

"Thank goodness, here at long last is a book that won't have any truck with the traditional show business pieties and hypocrisies. Michael Winner is thrillingly rude and forthright. Like Rhett Butler, he genuinely doesn't give a damn – and his book is hysterical." Roger Lewis, *Mail on Sunday*

320pp paperback, £9.99
Available now in all good bookshops or order from
www.therobsonpress.com